FRANCE
ALIVE

Claire Huchet Bishop

FRANCE
ALIVE

The Declan X. McMullen Co., Inc.
New York • 1947

To

my sister

who lives what I write

Contents

Preface

Of the courage, patience, fortitude and industry of the French people there have been ample reports. I saw them at first hand during the last two successive winters, and noted their remarkable advance even in that short period. This advance has been made so quietly and so ingeniously that the tremendousness of the effort has been partly concealed. The complete lack of ostentation has misled many outsiders, particularly those Americans who are more easily impressed by a noisier show of eagerness.

However, in America there have been many articles, even books, on France's material, intellectual and artistic "recovery" (if what we hear now in intellectual and artistic fields may be called "recovery" at all, for it never ceased to be very much alive even while underground). We have had similar valuable reports on the various phases of the political situation.

I have chosen, however, to speak of the living Christian spirit in contemporary France.

France's Christian renewal is a vast and varied subject. It touches Catholics, Protestants, Orthodox—in fact, all who are permeated by the Christian spirit. Thus, it pertains to all the activities of men in all walks of life. I make no attempt to cover the whole field, or even part of it, exhaustively. I wish only to give a modest account of what I have heard and seen. I trust that the reader will not be tempted either to generalize from my experiences or to minimize them, but merely to take them as indications of what is going on there.

But, fragmentary as is the picture in this book, it could not have been portrayed at all had it not been for the help of countless persons. To begin to record some of them by name would mean that too many would fail to receive rightful recognition. Still, I feel that a special word of thanks should go to the Dominicans who suggested much of my itinerary and showed so sympathetic an interest in my investigation that they gave me an inspired confidence. I wish also to express my gratitude to the clergy—regular and secular, Catholic and Protestant and Orthodox; to the members of many religious orders; to the lay people—believers and atheists alike; in fact, to all those throughout France who not only took pains to give me time and thought but who welcomed me with so much brilliance of intellect and generosity of heart. I cannot begin to do them justice; I can merely apologize for any failure on my part to present adequately their ideas and hopes and achievements.

Because my French friends engaged in the renewal have thought it best, I have refrained from using names of people and places, except where such omission would have proved too awkward. Although they are not in these pages by name, they are present by virtue of their spirit and effort.

A list of the works quoted and of other titles on the subject has been appended for all who wish to delve further into the extent of the renewal. This book, asked for by Americans and built of French materials, is intended only as a starting point for further and exciting adventures in perennial Christianity.

CLAIRE HUCHET BISHOP

May 19, 1947

FRANCE
ALIVE

Those Who Have
Come Back

IT IS ALWAYS MISLEADING TO try to segregate people into classes: those who have come back, those who stayed, those who fled. Human affairs are too interlocked. Still, a shared spiritual experience makes for a direct relationship. A lasting bond unites those men and women, for example, who have come back from concentration camps. They have told me repeatedly that they felt thoroughly at home only with those who had gone through such an experience. When they met in their local units they did not seek to identify each other as Catholics, Protestants, Jews, M.R.P., socialists or communists, but only as having been "there." "There" they had endured the same physical torments and experienced the reality of human communion. "There" they were all human beings, suffering persecution for justice's sake, or just suffering persecution. "There" they rediscovered and lived the communion

1

of the "faithful." They were kept alive by it, physically and mentally. They learned the efficacy of the bread of charity. Some of them knew that it was Christ; some did not. Now, many of them do not want to lose the fullness of that communion.

A Christian tells of how, when he was brutally snatched from the lineup by a German soldier to be beaten up because he had stumbled while walking, he heard his communist comrade whisper: "I'll pray for you." When he asked this atheist later how he could have said such a thing, he was answered: "You believe in it. So that was the only thing I could do for you at the time."

A priest tells of celebrating a clandestine Mass, with a Protestant serving and a communist keeping watch at the door.

A communist tells how he was surreptitiously supported in line for hours by his Christian companions during roll call, which, in winter, started at three o'clock in the morning. Anyone who could not remain standing was immediately shipped off and done away with. Unconcerned by the possibility of punishment, the Christians held up their friend despite their own weakness. He would have done the same for them.

People who have been through such things look at life in a stark, dynamic way. Approximately thirty thousand of them are organized in France. There are many more who have brought back this sense of the reality and power of communal spirit.

Returning from the horrors of Dachau, a village priest in Savoie is walking along the road and is heralded a few miles before he reaches his village. When he gets there, everybody is on the street to greet him, singing and praying. Flowers are thrown in his path; even the farm horses have been bedecked. The villagers all follow him into church. Still in his striped cotton prisoner's uniform, he ascends the pulpit: "Brethren, I, who come from the house of hate, tell you that only love can conquer hatred."

A Protestant minister, buried for months in solitary confinement, tells in the *Journal de Cellule* how he discovered the power of prayer, the reality of the communion of saints:

"One should not be surprised that prisoners learn to pray. . . . In prison, prayer is the whole life of the believer, particularly prayers of 'intercession'. . . . It seems one has to know sadness unto death in order to be able to ask with sufficient intensity that others be spared that sadness and that they be snatched out of despair and captivity. . . . The communion of saints. Miraculous presence. Marvelous prayer of the Didache. Yes, some day the Church will be one."

A Jew, taken to a concentration camp, refused to play the nazi game by acquiescing to the particularism of Israel. He was not officially a Christian, but he and his French Jewish companions were saturated with the Christian atmosphere of France, as he explains in *Le Camp de la Mort Lente*:

"How many French of Jewish origin are Christians without knowing it or without wishing it? . . . Even those to whom the Judaistic concept was very foreign, those even who felt Christian at heart, those who were Christians, did not refuse the Jewish label . . . On the human plan, solidarity was complete."

But the climate of Christian France had bred in this Jew and in his Christian companions the attitude of St. Paul: "neither Greek nor Jew." It had become a reality to them: "Three months of persecution, three months of physical and moral torture had not succeeded in giving me a Jewish soul."

His conclusion strangely echoes that of the Savoie priest: "Victim of hate, I remain convinced that nothing can be built on hate."

And this priest, who had chosen to be a factory worker among the French men and women conscripted by the Germans, who said Mass as he mixed mortar and gave Communion in a bathroom corner and absolution through barbed wire, says:

"By necessity we live a real communal life, where the exigencies of our Christianity are much clearer. Anything that is not absolutely necessary to us and that is needed by the other workers evidently does not belong to us any more, be it shirt, bread or money."

This sense of the oneness of human beings and of the effective power of communion, material and spiritual, permeates the attitude of many who have come back, be they war prisoners, political or racial deportees. The potent effect of spiritual charity is not a matter of words to them. They have it carved in their flesh. But the stigmas of suffering are also the stigmas of redemption. And they move about France, bearing Christ, consciously or unconsciously, through having been, themselves, living victims. The public demonstrations which have taken place, and are taking place, throughout France are but outward manifestations of an inner conviction so strong that it overflows.

I reported in the *Commonweal* of May 24, 1946, how I attended in a provincial town a Mass for the deportees who had died in Germany:

"A small chapel. Everyone who came was in mourning. The young priest who officiated said: 'A year ago I was working with my men in one of the tunnels for the rockets. We had only our striped cotton suits. It was below 32. We sabotaged as much as we could. At midnight, on Christmas, I managed to give Communion to my companions. I heard them in confession as we went on working. I kept the Host in a tiny tin box. At inspection I always managed to slip the box to the man who had just stripped before me and was dressing. It was never found. That Christmas of 1944, in that rocket tunnel, with the German guards around us, we felt boundlessly free. Christ was with us, right in that tunnel, and we knew there was victory though we be dead.' And he added bluntly and forcefully: 'Please come up, close, all of you, and let us *all* celebrate Mass. That we may not lose what we deportees, prisoners, *requis* found again: the Church of the bold, the martyrs, the saints.' "

Among those who served in the Resistance there are many who want to go on along the line of self-sacrifice and communal spirit they experienced with the *maquis*. I shall long remember the poignant intensity of the Memento of the Dead, said in French by a young priest who had been in the Resistance, as we gathered around him in a miserable back kitchen: "And, Lord, we pray for our comrades, who fell wondering if their deaths were of any use."

Mass was celebrated in Paris at the Palais de Chaillot (Trocadero) by Father Riquet, who had known Compiègne, Mauthausen, Dachau. Twenty thousand people participated. More than twelve thousand Communions were distributed. The number does not necessarily have significance, but it is an indication of France's state of mind that huge religious demonstrations take place: public, daring, popular demonstrations.

6

Recalling Fr. Riquet's heroic zeal during the war, J. J. Bernard, the well-known writer deported on racial grounds, has urged the necessity of holding firm to the Christian attitude as revealed and experienced in the camps:

"We have the illusion of being free, because the corset which constricted us has been loosened. Dangerous illusion. First we should become conscious of our limitations. Then we should rise above them through effort of the will and through *this movement of the soul* to which we are invited by those who have the mission to teach prisoners to look up beyond their horizon."

At Lourdes, in September 1946, there were one hundred thousand pilgrims, of all political shades, professions, and social strata, and from all parts of France. Many had walked great distances; others, still so weak from tortures, had to be wheeled. They had come in memory of the men and women who had sacrificed their lives. They had come to give thanks that they had survived. They had come to recapture the sense of human fraternity which they had discovered and lived amid the German hells.

"On Sunday morning, September 8th, at High Mass, from the entrance gate up to the Grotto is one great building. The altar on the dazzling white podium is the center around which the faithful gather, *circumscribus*, as the liturgy says. The wide lawn is the main aisle, filled with men; enthroned at the other end, the Teaching Church: cardinals and bishops. In the choir, those who are most precious to the assembly: the widows, the sick, and three symbolic graves. The sky of Lourdes serves as stained glass and vault.

"The Procession of the Holy Sacrament. These men have sung popular songs, but they know now how to keep silent. Here, so nearly forgotten nowadays, so well understood by the former prisoners: silence. This silent prayer of tens of thousands of men. 'Here, from the very moment you made your promise, Our Lady was waiting for you.' This astonishing silence is the measure of the seriousness of the gathering.

"It is the last evening. In the twinkling of an eye all the equipment of the camps, the gigantic numbers of the *Stalags*, the blue and red triangles, are torn away by the men. Some carry OFLAG IV D signs. STALAG III D, DACHAU and BERLIN proceed in the night. All the camp signs are triumphantly laid upon the podium under the glow of candlelight. The offering is made. It is already past.

"But it is not all idle emotion: 'Of our pilgrimage to the Blessed Virgin we want to make a manifestation, not of devotional piety, but of virile religion through the collective affirmation of our fearless determination to live as Christians.' "

And there, in front of Notre Dame de Lourdes,

many committed themselves to work, wherever they happened to be, for "the creation of a communal spirit, and to work with all their strength for social reforms."

For them it is not a matter of personal devotion or of personal salvation, but of the salvation of France and of the whole world, says H. Perrin:

"That which Our Father wants is not so much our own liberation and happiness—there is, of course, personal salvation—but the big business, the essential business, which towers above time, is the salvation of humanity, of the whole world. . . . Either we shall get out of a narrow and closed Christianity, a 'ghetto,' and boldly testify Christ, or else we shall disappear."

Thousands who have come back have committed themselves "boldly to testify Christ," not through words, but through deeds, through living that heroic and virile life which authentic Christianity calls for.

It is a privilege, a marked grace for France to have so many martyrs fired with Christian determination. It may be asked how, under the heading of Christians, I can speak in the same breath of baptized Christians, of Jews, of Communists. It is not from a sentimental, childish wish for "one happy family," nor is it a weak confusion of the issues. But those who have come back and want to consecrate themselves to the service of their brothers are militants, and in France there is less difference among a militant deportee Christian, a militant deportee communist and a militant deportee Jew than there is between a militant deportee Christian and a bigoted Christian. All of them, excepting the bigoted Christian, have been tortured and have lain at death's door for the sake of the commandment: "Thou shalt love thy neighbor as thyself." In the face of nazism, there has been a demonstration of faith in Christian values, whether labeled or not, unto death.

Barriers have been broken down. The communist has learned that Christianity is not clericalism. The Christian has learned that in *good* things he agrees with the communist: one cannot be for Christ and against the people. The Jew has found renewed support for his faith in French spiritual values, which are fundamentally Christian and agree with the most profound tenets of the faith of Israel. There is a new channel between the main currents of French life, an interchange, a mutual appreciation. They who have come back are the premises of the oneness of the Kingdom.

Christianity of Life

IN SPEAKING OF THE CHRIS-
tian aspect of the renewal in France, I find I have first
to contend with a prevailing attitude.

It is not a Protestant fear that this book may deal
with Catholicism only, since France is primarily a Catholic country. I shall, on the contrary, speak of the whole
Christian renewal, Catholic and Protestant.

It is not a Jewish indifference to the Christian outlook, because, in the words of His Holiness, Pope Pius
XI, "We Christians are Semites spiritually."

Nor is it the communist challenge that "religion is
the opiate of the people," because militant communists
in France have learned in the concentration camps that
authentic Christianity is not such.

No, the difficulty, which stands in the way like a
mountain before I can make the American reader grasp
what is happening in France, is the place usually attrib-

uted to religion in the life of man. So that, when I speak of the spiritual renewal in France, every reader, whether Catholic, Protestant, Jew or communist, will expect things connected with religion and not with life. Many people divorce the spiritual and the temporal, granting that there is a time and place for each. To them, religion is all a little boring; at best, a side issue. Some people, they say, may have the disposition to be more interested, but for us there are the "important" problems: the cost of living, Russia, the stock market, the rights of unions and the atomic bomb.

This is not surprising. When have we seen Christians who have not had two lives, one temporal, one spiritual; one for business days, one for Sunday? Some, who call themselves Christians, insist: "We try to bring a certain amount of ethics into our daily lives. We do not actually put our hand into our neighbor's pocket; we do not murder him in cold blood. We do not go quite so far as actually to commit adultery. There is an amazing number of things we don't do because we are Christians." And that, say the French Christians I have met, is just the trouble: negative, weak, emasculated Christianity. It is not the Christianity Our Lord brought when the crowd followed Him day and night, even when He was not performing miracles. It is not the Christianity which inspired the longshoremen of Corinth and the workers of Rome and the tough bar-

barians. To be a Christian is *to do* something. And the "doing" is *to be*—everywhere and anywhere—not by sentimental declarations, but by a way of being, a determination to look at all things in the light of Christianity.

"To be a Christian is to astonish," say the French. And they add: "There is no such thing as being a solitary Christian. Christianity is a communal affair." Some may say that these are old truths. They are. The main point is to live them again, and not simply to know them with the intellect. Many French are living them again. The virile realization that they are members of Christ colors their whole daily life. This is the core of the whole French renewal: a dynamic Christianity which is a communal affair.

We shall see that this allegiance leads the French into bold spiritual-temporal adventures, if we may use such a term in order to view the two ideas in their oneness. The accent of these Christians is not on protecting themselves from personal falls (old style: "How to save my soul"; new style: "I have to save the souls of my brothers."), but in venturing with heart and will and intelligence into the avenues of fraternal relationship.

We often hear in America that "the communists are everywhere." I dare say the same thing could be said in France. But it also can be said that "the Christians are everywhere": in the factories, the fields, the

13

universities, the shops, the banks, in high and low places and, perchance, in churches, too!

Some may ask why we do not see the results in politics and economics. The answer is, partly, because worth-while things take time in France, and partly because all the efforts are not centralized. (There are some extremely good points and some bad ones in the fact that there is not complete centralizing of effort.) Another reason is that Christianity is acting, as it always acts on civilization, as a leaven to raise the dough. There is not only the leaven. There is also the dough.

How did it all start? This rethinking of Christianity in terms of modern man has been coming for a long time. Christianity is always basically the same, but it wears different clothing in different nations and in different centuries. And when one says that Christianity is the same, one does not mean that it is static. The message is the same, but the deciphering goes on through the ages. That is why the Church is both immutable and endlessly young. And just now it is her perennial youthfulness that is bursting forth all over France. It seems almost as if it might be too late, were not the fervor so deep.

The divorce of the Church from the people started about a century ago, although there were signs, even before that, of misunderstanding. Distrust between priest and people had steadily deepened; the clergy had more and more identified itself with the bourgeois, in spite of the encyclicals, and the workers were shunning the clergy, who did not seem to be with them and often were not. Catholicism became synonymous with reaction and capitalistic exploitation.

Yet, in the midst of the bog where French Catholicism seemed content to lie, there were, even as far back as 1890, authentic Catholics whose "salt had not lost its savor." The first who should be mentioned are Albert de Mun and Léon Bloy. It is not my intention to prepare a historical study of the pioneers of the present renewal. But it is most doubtful whether the French renewal would be what it is today had not those people fought for Catholicism with bitter passion over fifty years ago. The Association Catholique de la Jeunesse Française, ancestor of the JOC, was a student movement which in 1886 was defined by the organizer, Albert de Mun, a sincerely Catholic bourgeois, in these terms: "The object of the ACJF is to restore Christian social order. You [the students] are Catholics; you are engaged to serve the Church. Never forget that by this fact you are also engaged to serve the poor and the weak; *you are of necessity with the people.*"

But the fiercest blow struck at the slumbering Catholics came from Bloy.

"His atheist father had not deemed it necessary to oppose this empty sham of religious instruction which excuses for priests, stuffed with formulas, squeeze out like dirty seminary linen over young, uninterested foreheads. . . . Memory and imagination had simply received this vague, *literal* mark of Christian symbolism which sacrilegious entrepreneurs consider sufficient for granting the certificate preliminary to Holy Eucharist. It was only later—ten years later—that, having skimmed through the New Testament for the first time while idly warming his feet during a night watch in 1870, he had the immediate, crushing perception of divine Revelation."

Bloy's love for Christianity was unbounded, violent, aggressive. He had been snatched body and soul by Christ, without any lessening of his intelligence or shadowing of his powerful physical nature. He would not stand for any emasculation of the message of Christ. For twenty-five years his passionate invectives, his red-blooded love-insults fell on bourgeois Catholicism. Bloy died in poverty and misery, ignored by the anti-religious, despised by most of the religious. Twenty years after his death, Stanislas Fumet wrote: "He was to engender many children in the faith. . . . One can well picture Léon Bloy becoming the ancestor of passionate, tender, bold, faithful Christians."

The passionate, tender, bold, faithful Christians are in France now, and the fact that there are so many priests among them would be a great joy to Bloy. "He

16

wanted the great Church of his heart to be alive, and nothing made him suffer more than the priests' torpor."

The torpor is gone. Of course, one should not expect all the Catholics in France—priests, monks, sisters and laymen—to "astonish" one, or all the churches to be communities of the faithful. One probably will meet more priest-administrators and formalist Catholics and enter more "dead" churches than one will meet dynamic Christians or enter lively, communal churches. Yet, these fresh sources are welling up all over France in a hundred ways. One may stumble on some of these actively Christian people, on one of these churches, on one of these nun factory-workers, on one of these Christian economic ventures. And, perchance, if you are very quiet, if they sense your sincerity, they may say something about it all. But they are all "dead against" publicity. "We are not guinea pigs. We are not experimenting. We are just living. Living Christianity. A Christianity of Life."

The torpor is gone, all along the line, from the topmost hierarchy to the least curate, straight through the lay people. It may be a cardinal, long seasoned in the Church, or a prizefighter who is just learning how to pray, a scientist or a scrubwoman. They do not separate Christianity from life. Christianity informs their very lives, whether it be higher mathematics or the shoveling of coal in a mine—one stupendous resetting of the whole world tapestry on the Christian loom.

Of course, this does not at all mean that there is nothing but action, with no place for contemplative life. This would end in moralism and a weakening of religious values. The contemplative life and religious values take on added import through keen perception of the world's needs. But it means that for all, Christianity has become inseparable from living dangerously —because it is a total engagement.

Of the many flowerings of the renewal, I have selected only a few characteristics. I could not begin to see everything and meet everybody. And there are some fields, such as the intellectual and the artistic life,* education and matrimony, which I had to leave deliberately aside. I had to limit myself to a few main aspects, which alone proved so exhaustive that I have had to sift considerably. What remains will, I hope, suffice to illustrate this "Christianity of Life," which is embraced by people of all classes, but most readily by the common man. In my enthusiasm at finding a Christianity so alive that it

* I cannot refrain from mentioning the church in Savoie which is being decorated by the greatest French artists, who have been asked deliberately to contribute to the making of a house of God, thereby to bring Christian art back into the lively current of modern art. Fernand Léger is doing the mosaic for the façade; Lurçat is making the tapestry; and Derain Bracque is working, too. The altars are decorated by Bonnard and the stained glass is the achievement of Ronault and of Fr. M. A. Couturier, who is well known in the United States and in Canada.

could inflame factory workers, I spoke to a friend of what I had seen. And she, not being a communist deportee, but only a fellow-traveler, remarked calmly: "The Church is clever. She sees that the masses have fallen away from her. So now she has changed her methods."

The Workers in Action

THERE IS NO DENYING THAT there are grounds for support of my friend's remark by atheists and Protestants in France. I suppose that even the honesty of recognizing the legitimacy of the criticism will also be set down as utmost cleverness. One simply cannot get out of it with words! The active French Catholics know that distrust. They understand it, and how, through the very fault of Catholics, it has come to be so. They do not waste time denying or explaining. They know there is only one thing that will break down the wall: friendship. But their friendship is not a scheme, not a means of getting people back into the Church. Some workers are distrustful of Christian friendship, which they consider only as bait. No, this Christian friendship is the service of Christ *per se,* therefore an end in itself. The French insist on this over and

over again. The aim of their efforts is, in the words of
F. Boulard:

"Not to make mere church-goers; not the 'salvation' of each individual; not the foundation of a new
Christianity. The great revelation of Christianity is its
incarnation in daily life. . . . The final sign, the one
Christ gave us, is charity toward neighbor through love
of God: By that sign you will be known as My disciples,
if you love one another. . . . Supernatural life is not an
outer garment . . . but a deep transformation of the
whole man. In other words, supernatural life should
transform natural life: the love of God should blossom
into love of neighbor. Then, and then only, has the
pagan evolved into a Christian. All Christianity is incarnated in life."

Against tremendous odds, comparable to those en-
countered by the first Christians—perhaps even greater,
since they are in the midst of a people which has known
and forgotten Christianity—the French Christians have
set out to live the life of Christ, the life of friendship.

A healthy girl of twenty from an industrial town
once stood before me, radiant. She spoke as if the "new
style" of Christianity were an everyday matter.

"Well, I don't know where I shall sleep next."

"Haven't you a home?"

"I used to live with my mother. But my mother is
old, she's forty-five, and it wasn't fair to her to keep

open house day and night. You know what I mean: when you're a Christian you have to do that, of course. So I went to share a place with a girl friend of mine who was also a Christian, and we could keep open house. Sometimes even the kitchen was packed with people sleeping on the floor. Then my friend left town, and I took another place. But Father 'X' came along, and he had no place to go. So I said: 'I'll move out and you can have this place. It's easier for me to find something, because I've lived in this town all my life and you haven't.' But the place I let him have wasn't much of a proposition! Because by that time all I had left was practically only what I had on my back. You know, if you're a Christian, you don't possess anything."

"Where will you go?"

"Oh, I don't worry! You see, there are lots of Christian homes around now, communal families, all helping each other out of friendship. That's among the converts mostly. When they marry, they make their homes communal homes."

"And when did you become a Christian?"

"My father didn't believe. No one did in our family. But my father was a wonderful man—what they call a humanitarian. We were in the Resistance, and were both captured by the Germans. In prison someone gave me a New Testament and after that I could not think of anything else except that 'someone had died for us out of love.' And my father had made the same discovery in his prison, only I didn't know it until I got out. They shot my father, but he had been able to let my mother know what had happened to him in prison—that he had become a Christian. And I went to church, where I had never been before, and told the priest I wanted to become a Christian, too. And I guess we just did not understand each other at all. But I was baptized and made my first Communion. Then I went to church every Sunday, and I tried to understand the sermons. But I couldn't. I was very unhappy, because I could not see the connection between what had happened to my father and to me and what they were talking about in church. But all those dreary months I kept going and saying to God: 'It must be that I am stupid. Please, God, send me someone to explain.' Of course, I had understood right away that, if you are a Christian, nothing belongs to you, that you must be always, always ready to share. That's evident. And I started living like that right away. But I felt lonely in church. Even going to Communion, which was so great an experience, was lonely. It was as if the Christians who went to receive did it singly. It was not 'we Christians' all together, not the community. Then Father 'X' came. It was wonderful. He understood everything. He works in a factory himself. And since Father lives with us we have had our Mass; it's truly the communion of us all,

all together. Father explains everything. And there are more and more Christian communities starting all over town. We have no money, except what we earn, but it is amazing! Truly, if you rely on God He does not let you down. You know how it is to be a Christian."

And her ardent, gentle, courageous face glowed with happiness. I felt the tears coming to my eyes: this familiar and affectionate friendship, this complete confidence that I, too, know what it is to be a Christian. But do I? And do I feel the same pride and joy as this factory girl does when I say that I am a Christian?

The term "Christian" is the only one, beside "communist," which still carries a challenge in France. To be a Christian still is fresh, interesting, annoying or sympathetic, and, whatever the reaction, is always accompanied with respect. There was a time when it was not so. Christianity was linked with lack of intelligence, fearful minds, closed vision. Now, even the old anticlerical slogans fall short with the people. They have seen Christians with outstanding intelligence, fearless Christians, farsighted ones. To be a Christian is something in France nowadays. It is not an administrative label. It is the sign of friendship unto death, the friendship which comes from a vivid belief in "Our Father."

Frequently, the dynamic and communal Christian message takes root through a disciple of Albert de

24

Mun or Bloy, or through a grandson of a *Silloniste* of 1905 who obediently submitted to the decision of the Church at the time, but did not give up looking and praying for a renewal which would have the approval of the whole Church, or through someone who has been a Jocist or whose son is one today.

Though the JOC (Jeunesse Catholique Ouvrière) is now twenty years old, it should be talked about here because it is still very active. It is the concrete answer to Pope Pius XI's famous declaration: "The great scandal of the Church in the nineteenth century is not that she lost so many workers, but that she lost the working class." One man in the 1920s was so deeply conscious of that fact that he dedicated his life to the cause. The son of a miner, he had a burning love for the working class and for Christ. And he knew that the two were made for each other. He was Abbé Cardijn of Belgium. He knew that "the doctrine of Christ does not scare the proletariat, but what throws them off is the way we present it." He started to take some young men into his confidence. It was not a matter of getting them together in a group outside the factory or the mine, nor of corralling them into the Church; rather, it was a matter of waking them up to Christian life right where they were, in the mine or in the factory. The slogan was, "See, judge and do something about it."

In 1927, at Clichy in Paris, the French JOC started

with four young workers and a priest. The JOC now numbers four hundred thousand in France, not counting, of course, all those who have gone through the JOC, are now married and still are engrossed in "being" Christians.

The great originality of the JOC lay in its bold unearthing of the dynamism of the Christian message and in its endless adaptations of the message to the workers' state. The face of Christ the worker had imposed itself upon Cardijn with such force that he could make it alive with revolutionary intensity in the minds of the young workers. In France, if the young worker was an athletic fellow and clever, even quite brazen, about Christ, so much the better. Soon, others became interested, because the fellow was not only "regular," but was more than that. And other "toughs" wanted to know why. In his own words he would tell them he had given himself to a cause. That they could understand. And he would tell them it was Christ's cause. Christ was his "boss." And some of them would say that it was all a child's bedtime story, and that they were "fed up" long ago with the Church. Others did not know anything at all about Christ, so he would tell all about Him in his own words. Here is an authentic sample of impromptu "presentation," as reported by H. Godin:

"I have discovered a regular pal: Christ the worker, a pal above board, for good and for bad days. I learned that, far from being an inaccessible God, he was born in a stable, a real one. That for thirty years he had sweated and worked hard enough to get calluses on his hands. Thirty years of the slavery of that time without the forty-hour week and a paid vacation. That he revolutionized the world as a leader of men, with twelve helpers he chose. He got his point of view over, the ideal he had come to bring to the workers of this earth. The guy who met him was won over. He was some leader. He was not afraid to talk to the street women in order to save them, and he put in his place the fat millionaire who reproached him for his friends. He said: Love one another, help one another. The old bigoted woman who speaks evil of her neighbor the minute she comes out of church? A counterfeiter. The so-called Christian boss who has less consideration for his workers than for his machines? A piece of junk. And too many of those who go to chuch, and whose life is nothing but wickedness, egoism and injustice? *Ersatz* Christians."

It was not easy to be a friend of Christ the worker in the factory, to stand for justice, fair wages, vacations, insurance, human treatment, right on through in allegiance to Christ's admonition: "Love thy neighbor as thyself," and at the same time to stand firm against any demagogy, which is lack of respect for the human person. The management did not like you, because you were a vital, active reproach. Or sometimes they did like you, and that was worse, because they imagined that, since you were a Catholic, they could use you to further their own ends. And, if the other workers did come to acknowledge that you were one of them in their claims, even if it were for a different aim, at the same time they would still distrust you because too many Catholics, high ones especially, had crucified Christ the worker long ago and put in his place a sweet, sugary, papier-mâché figure.

To be a Jocist in those days in France often meant to be beaten up and left as good as dead on the sidewalk. As the Jocists grew in number, respect increased. And some of them were toughs, who put the good fists the Lord had given them into His service. But the opposition lost its violent character after the Armistice: many Jocists were in the Resistance. Many were deported. Some, who had been conscripted by the Germans, were later sent to concentration camps because of their Christian testimony and died there. Some of the *maquis* were shot. All of them had borne their Christian testimony to the limit of their understanding and to its ultimate consequence.

The way the Jocists have carried on their activity has been extremely varied, original and somewhat disconcerting to the average bourgeois mentality. Besides their relentless fight for workers' rights, there have been dozens of startling initiatives:

"During the winter of 1941-42, which was so hard on babies, the 'strong-minded ones' of 'A' tore away the wool coats from the pet dogs taken out walking on the boulevards by their 'mothers,' and brought them in triumph to the National Aid.

"It is in black marketing that Leon has completely won over Jules and André to Christ. And you can be sure that, when the 'section' wants to throw a little party, nothing is lacking . . ."

"A team decides to go to the clandestine balls and dance with all the girls who are not good-looking and who get discouraged.

"A tough gang does not give up fighting, but wants to fight for Christ, so they tear to pieces all the dirty magazines on the magazine stands in their quarter.

That is what it means to be a "band of the friends of Christ," as some Jocists put it. To be ready to do anything for Christ's sake, with the tremendous lift given by His companionship. Christ was a worker. "Workers, be proud!" "We Christians." The Revolution—that's us!"

It would be wrong to give an idea of the JOC as a movement organized along fixed rules. It is ever moving, ever inventing and improvising. The initiatives, as in all Catholic action in France, comes from the bottom up. The committees centralize and sift the many sug-

29

gestions which emanate from the local units, and which may eventually become national programs. It may be a concerted effort along economic lines, as, for instance, the insistence that it become legal to have a young representative of the apprentices and younger groups in the factory at the councils of labor. Or it may be the study of the Gospel along certain lines. Whatever it be, the initiative starts from below, and the cohesive work of the committees is only to give adequate expression to the general interest or wish.

This starting from below is extremely important, because it gives the proper Christian direction to the whole effort. Without it, the whole thing is but a maneuvering of the masses: "to reach the mass and not to be preoccupied with its development." This conception is justifiable among people who do not believe in the glorious destiny of man, or that he is ordained to God. But the authentic Christian effort can only help the masses to come of age, so that they might be their own masters, masters of their duties and responsibilities, free men and not the slaves of self-centered capitalistic economy, not the passive beneficiaries of a paternal one, nor the servants of the State or of the Party. The Christian respect for all human beings is there. The Christians do not wish to force powerfully, and often disdainfully, some economic, political or cultural advantage upon the workers. They want them to work out their own salvation in the fullest sense of the word. And in the end many French workers prefer that. They are quick to say: "The capitalist was the boss. Now the Party wants to be the boss. It's always bosses. We are tired of bosses."

Not only do young factory workers and miners become Christians, but also those who work at unclassified jobs—circus people, boxers, street vendors, garbage collectors, a motley of turbulent, devil-may-care young people. A prize fighter, usually surrounded by a crowd of admiring young people, was converted, and he used to undress rapidly on the boulevard and, wearing only trunks, climb up a lamp post in the evening to preach the Gospel which he had just discovered! His success, of course, was tremendous. His explanations were colorful and spicy, and he always ended by challenging anyone to fight out his arguments. Of course, no one ventured a word! But many young men, very much impressed, followed him to the feet of Christ. They and the others like them were absolutely sincere, and they were most eager to learn to look at all their problems through Christ. And, if they insisted on practical solutions, they were unstinting in their heroism. Their generosity and unbounded enthusiasm were certainly nearer Christ's heart than the selfish little devotions of

"Christians" of long standing. Abbé Godin, speaking of his section in Paris, said:

"Oh, it was chaotic and disconcerting: they brought to Mass all the fellow travelers (and what fellow travelers!). It was to them a kind of demonstration. All those who made their first Communion would come to receive. They knew they received Christ ('The Great Caid'), and they prayed to Him with the naivete of first communicants. But, to facilitate the conquest of their buddies, they did not hesitate to go and have a drink before Mass with them: 'Since it is not for pleasure, but for charity,' they said. They did not become saints all at once. They fell often, but they got up again in a total offering of themselves to Christ."

And their total offering goes hand in hand with the pride of their affirmation: "The apostles—that's us!"

The JOC has helped many young workers to come of age. And in the weekly gatherings in kitchen or attic, to which they have invited the chaplain, they have thrashed out all the big problems—not only economic problems, but the problems of love, of religion, of the destiny of man. They have ravenously fed on the Gospel; they discuss it, offer free and startling commentaries and take to it fervently and to the letter.

A few years ago an edition of the Gospel was made by the JOC. Here is the reproduction of the title page:

The largest printing in the world
The largest reading in the world
The largest influence in the world

GOOD NEWS

or

Infallible method to be happy and at
peace
brought by CHRIST JESUS, called

GOSPEL

by

Matthew, tax collector, apostle, first
witness;

Mark, propagandist, secretary to St.
Peter;

Luke, physician and man of learning,
associate of St. Paul;

John, fisherman, apostle, first witness.

The authors of this book have accepted
martyrdom to guarantee their testimony.
This book challenges all learned men to
be found at fault, according to the most
recent documentary research, either for
its data or its complete veracity.

And here are a few of the Jocist reactions to the Gospel, in such outspoken language that it may scare many readers, French and American:

Of the Annunciation:

"You must have been a honey of a girl, lively, not shy, not silly. Modern. Ah, I wish I could have seen the good girls of the parish confronted by such a proposition! What a fuss they would have made! They would have said, 'I am not worthy.' . . . Those girls! You would have seen their scandalized look, you would have heard them protesting: 'We don't understand what you are talking about, because we are virtuous girls, so we don't know how children are born.' That's what they would have said, the ones we know. But that little one, she speaks simply. She says simply what she thinks, without any fuss. Ah, what heart she must have had, that little one! . . ."

Of the thirty years at Nazareth:

"I would never have thought that Christ had been a worker, considering the Church is against the workers."

"The Church is the Society of Christians, the Society of those who are for Christ, and Christ was a worker. So how can you say that the Society is against Christ? Look at Christ's life, at those He loved best, and at those who made Him die, then you will know what Christ thought of workers."

"The Church, in preaching resignation, is against the workers, because she prevents them from revolting against their misery and their slavery, and she has always made a lot of the good-for-nothings who have money."

"And who was the first one to defend the workers and say they should have a decent salary? Leo XIII, a Pope, and Pius XI, another Pope. There has been a good deal of social progress, but it has not come up yet to those Encyclicals."

"You are O.K. And the Pope, and the JOC, but all Catholics do not follow the Pope."

"The soldiers who do not march with the army are deserters, that's all. It's true there are lots of people who call themselves Christians and who are not."

"Yes, those people do harm."

"Sure, and you, you are more Christian than they are."

"If Christ is really like that . . . if you are not trying to pull my leg . . ."

Since the war the JOC has kept on moving and learning. There is a tendency not to make so much of the word "Jocist," which sounds like a label, and to use the term "Christian." The direction, in the communal Christian sense, has affirmed itself: not to make a grouping of young people against another grouping of young people.

The main thing seems just *to be*. To be a Christian everywhere, in the factory, at home, during leisure time. To be the leaven in the dough. Not solitarily, but communally. The kitchen talks and the outings are open to anyone, and there is no effort to make other people join. Only friendship: "that they be one, so that the world believe that Thou has sent me." Not a sentimental friendship, but an effective one which brings material, intellectual and moral liberation. The priests wait to be asked to the get-togethers and outings. And, if they are not asked, they don't worry. They know that, if they truly deserve the title of "Father," the time will come when they will be asked and, likely, to such an extent that they might fear the burden were it not for Christ's help.

All the Jocists I met were anxious about America. What kind of JOC was America going to have? "Tell them," they said, "that they will have to find the formula which suits their own country. Tell them to have moral activity not *against*, but *for*."

CHAPTER FOUR

The Communal Family

O UT OF THE JOC THE MPF
(Mouvement Populaire des Familles) was born. Seeking to find its way since the late 1930s, it has now come
into its own because of the inefficiency of successive
governments. The workers have taken over. The MPF
is free of all political affiliation. Politics is never discussed, and no one cares. As a member of the MPF explained to me: "Workers can always agree on fraternal
realizations: (1) No paternalism (boss, State or Party);
(2) The will to act; (3) The welfare of the family, but
not in a narrow sense; (4) The welfare of the community. It is on that, and not on the bad instincts, that
one can build." The title, MPF, is somewhat misleading.
It groups everyone, including bachelors and widows.
There is absolutely no barrier. The only requisite is that
a member be a worker, that is, have a small salary and
(or) insecurity. Some manual workers, for instance,

may not enter the category, and some intellectuals may.

The MPF is free of church ties. There are rank and file communists who are perfectly content in the MPF, as well as militant Catholics. Everyone knows that this movement for mutual help and justice was born out of Christian concern and gets its inspiration from the Christian spirit. Christian ideology is there, and it is not antipathic, even to the communist. Many workers are communists because it is called the party of the workers, and it seems a sort of treason not to belong to it. But it does not follow necessarily that one adopts dialectical materialism and dictatorship. Nor does it follow that God is to be thrown overboard. To people who have breathed the air of France for a long time, it all seems a little oversimplified. But they do like the idea of taking things over, and the MPF provides for such a course. It does not try to form an elite among the masses, but it works in such a way that the masses enjoy progress from the inside, of themselves.

There is no talking for its own sake in MPF. One starts right away doing something. And the initiative arises from below; the leaders are only executives of the people's wishes. The grouping is by quarter, by street, by house, always by neighborhood units. Thus, the MPF, like all the new Christian efforts, works toward the disappearance of the proletariat, through its own internal efforts. For a proletarian is basically someone uprooted, who has no community ties. In the MPF there is practically no administration. There are no funds outside the fraternal collections. If a neighborhood group decides to have a party for the old people of the quarter, everyone gets busy baking and sewing. Another group supports one of its members in a sanatarium for a year. During the war all the members would go en masse to a bombed-out house to find shelter for the families, and later help them start housekeeping again; each member would bring something—a chair, a mattress, a kettle—truly sharing to the limit of his ability. Small cooperatives are started, run by the members during leisure hours. They pool their resources toward a vacation in the country. It is endless. The individualistic French have learned they can no longer have, by their own efforts alone, the things they want. If they still loathe collectivism, yet they are deeply responsive to the life of friendship. I remember the indignant comment of a young Christian who had gone to visit a sick person in her street: "Just think! She thought I was a social worker! Isn't that horrible? I told her I was a neighbor, a *neighbor!*"

The life of friendship does not go on without difficulties. In the winter of 1946-47, all over France, the sections of the MPF were faced with the problems of homeless families—no place to go, everybody crowded to the limit, nothing to rent. The members of the MPF saw to it that the families filled in all the proper forms and went through the required red tape. Then, when all this was done, they went to the government office, talked things over and said: "We warn you that, if by this date you have not taken care of these people, we shall occupy such and such a house which has been empty for so long. . . ." And they did it. The huskiest men took charge, moved the few belongings, secured the key to the empty house, and, if they could not get it, broke in the door as gently as possible! Then they installed the homeless families. They tried to have four or six together, because this made it more difficult for the authorities who might have sought to dispossess them. Eventually, the police arrived. The huskier members stood at the door, and the police, usually, understanding the predicament of mothers and babies, were content with writing out a summons. A trial did not come up for weeks, and, when it came, the government either arranged for the people to stay where they were or found another place for them.* On a few occasions, some overzealous policemen clashed with the husky neighbors. They found it hard going. The MPF members stood their ground vigorously, even though they were left in poor shape. Surprised at the readiness of supposedly mild people to defend their rights, the police

* Since this was written, word has been received that some courts have decided against the squatters.

40

retreated and wrote the usual summons. The MPF counterattacked by bringing suit against the city government.

The MPF members are not hotheaded. They do not relish disturbances or fights. But they do believe in helping one another, not through big, anonymous methods, but in a just, effective and fraternal way.

They give their full support to any communal activity in their respective quarters. The quarter includes, of course, *all* the inhabitants, not only the official members of the MPF. One becomes a member almost automatically the moment one starts doing something for others in the neighborhood. It follows naturally that, among people who keep working for the communal good, ideas of communal activities germinate: not only social communal affairs, but also communal work enterprises. The idea of communal work originally had nothing to do with the MPF, but it found favorable soil, since the MPF was so familiar with communal social enterprises. So, there are communal laundries, communal printing shops, communal home service. Home service was devised for women with children who needed temporary aid. The MPF believes that, though a woman should be left free to work outside, it is the communal duty to help her at home, so that the whole community does not slide into collectivism (nurseries, families eating out, etc.) which, since it kills the *Christian* sense of man, kills the *whole* sense of man.

The MPF illustrates very effectively Canon Tiberghien's masterful saying: "No fishing with a line, no fishing with a net, but changing the water of the pond." We should think along such lines in considering the Catholic effort in France. Everything is done locally, but with a keen sense of the universal. The masculine conception of Christianity, with all its vigor and breadth, merges with the feminine side, expressed in daily, intimate contacts. The two are absolutely inseparable.

Integration of Christian spirit in community life appears most clearly, perhaps, in a town in the south of France, where the effort is carried out on three plans, directed by teams, called the Team of Structures, the Resident Team and the Sacerdotal Team.

The duties of the team of structures are to study and reform living conditions among the workers, methods of hiring labor and ways of organizing work. Laymen with a bent for such problems and with sound technical knowledge of them, who are willing to go on studying them, can enter this field. It is a field for Christian economists, architects, city planners and labor organizers. Of course, the people must be able to support themselves and their families outside this work. Such planning is not new. Many people have devoted their lives to it, and some good has been accomplished. But what characterizes the Christian effort in this particular town is this. It is not one organization opposed to another organization. The people operate within existing organisms, and the results of their studies and work are available to all. Plans already have been adopted by the Municipal Council and the CGT—which had been widely explained by the team of structures, *"Economie et Humanisme."* The team works in close connection with the resident and sacerdotal teams, which we shall examine later. Thus, the study of conditions from the economic point of view is not divorced from human contact with those who suffer from existing conditions, and with those especially concerned with the inner life of man. It is a specialization which never loses sight of the whole man.

Resident teams have other tasks. Years ago social workers had started to bring help and counsel to the working population. But the movement soon degenerated into a succession of huge organizations built upon little more than a lot of papers and red tape. Besides, the social worker was always an outsider, not a neighbor who shared the life of the people. It soon became an anonymous activity through which one could get something.

The Christian Residents, however, make their home

in the midst of the people, especially among those un-protected by the law. They do it because they believe that nothing can take the place of sharing the same life, difficulties, sorrows, joys, daily routine and common destiny. They do it in order to give better social help. They do it to be *present*, living representatives of Christian brotherhood.

But, above all, they do it "because they are haunted by the idea of participating in the disappearance of this well-defined sickness which is called proletarianism." Their concern is "the material, intellectual and moral liberation of the proletariat from within, through daily helping of one another." Thus, the Christian Residents, by participating in the same destiny, are the means of bringing about the disappearance of the economic and psychological causes of the very existence of the pro-letariat.

"The Residence," M. R. Loew clarifies, "is not a sport, nor a record of visits, counsels, surgical dressings and needles. It is not merely a work of love and a gift of one's one physical strength. It should be a *work of the mind*. It is not only the daily struggle against the physical and moral misery of the quarter; it is a par-ticipation in the great movements of human civiliza-tion, particularly the workers' movement."

In order to keep a proper perspective and not to become absorbed in daily work to the point of being swallowed up by it, it has seemed imperative that the Residents live as teams. A team of three seems to work well, since three are enough to be helped by one another's spiritual companionship and not enough to be hampered by material over-organization. The resident team remains in frequent, often daily, contact with the teams of structures. In that way the work of each has root in concrete reality, the team of structures profiting from the practical knowledge of the daily contacts of the resident team, and the resident team keeping its head well above the sea of details because of its contact with the team of structures.

The Residents take their place in the quarter. Sometimes they all work outside; sometimes one or two of them, and if possible they take turns making a living for the team. Their home is like the other homes of the quarter. All help given remains on the level of the good neighbor. It may include delousing a child, making a surgical dressing, getting papers for a foreigner, going to the police to get a child out of a scrape, or praying at a wake. It may include explaining how to go about getting insurance, how to get into a sanatarium, how to send the child to a camp. Those are all the things a neighbor can do, informally, intimately. It is really endless, and the presence of a residence acts as a catalyzer for the whole quarter. For Christ said: "Where two or three are gathered in my name, I am

among them." It is not sufficient to be gathered, ag-
glomerated, placed in juxtaposition; it has to be in His
name. Around the home of the Residents, the house of
friendship, lines of forces come gradually to converge,
to be an organic pattern. It takes a Christian community, even of only two or three, to "precipitate" the
formation of crystals in an hitherto unorganized body,
making it gradually alive from within and for eternity,
the "now" and the future manifestation of St. John:
"For now we are the sons of God and it does not yet
appear what we shall be but we know that at the time
of that manifestation we shall be like him because we
shall see him as he is."

Throughout France there are many ways of being
a Resident. The names vary in different places: Residents, Women of the Mission of France, Teams, Para-
teams. And in each case the work is handled differently,
according to the conditions and the temperament of
those who undertake it. In several districts the women
hold in common not only the money they earn, but even
their personal belongings.

They do not constitute an order; they take no
vows; they dress like other women; their promises of
obedience, chastity and poverty are made only to the
team itself; they answer only to their confessor. Their
period of "noviceship" lasts for eight months, during
which they are supervised by a priest-worker. For this

46

period they reorganize their lives completely—education, speech, manners—so that they will give no offence to those among whom they live.

In some places they are fortunate enough to have found a miserable abode for themselves, living along as a team of three. Elsewhere, they have had to move in with families. To carry on their work, to answer the call successfully, it is necessary for one to have reached a state of mind where one does not think to have something to give, but to receive from these truly miserable people.

The members of the teams come from all walks in life. As some of them are from wealthy families, they bring their trousseau and jewels when they join. The trousseau is divided among the team and the surplus is carefully put aside for needy callers. Some of the jewels are sold for the care of the needy, and some are kept for any of the girls to wear when they go to the neighborhood Saturday dances. They had been quick to notice that in the factory, though the other women were friendly, they considered them apart, and this was because they had not been going to the dances in the quarter. So they dressed up and went, always three together. Then they were finally "accepted."

One team was once awakened in the middle of the night by six Spanish refugees, who had no place to go. The girls hesitated a bit. But they decided that, after all, they could not possibly leave them outside. So they moved their few belongings to the next floor and gave the first floor to the refugees for the night. The refugees stayed six months—and they ate, too. But that was what the team's home was for: to be used. And it is used, constantly; they always have surprise guests around their table: boxing champions, technicians, communists, Dominicans.

Then there is another team that lives in a boarding house occupied by prostitutes, who were turned out of the *maisons de tolérance* under the new law. The team has made real friends with them. They all go together to the movies and the theater, they take walks together, they read and sew together as all girls do. Friendship, Christ's spirit.

And there are the teams that live and work and share a common destiny, not with the proletariat, but with the subproletariat, those pathetic people who have been deadened in body and soul by years of mechanical work, or by too strenuous physical work (the women especially). There exists an army of subproletarians, the refuse of society, about whom not even the unions or the communist party bothers. They live in hovels and ramshackle huts, and they labor all day under the factory foreman's watch—as deadly a weapon as the whip of the Pharaohs' overseers. Many of these people live in worse than animal degradation. They have lost all power of thought. They react only to the lowest forms of physical pleasure. Humanity has been drained out of them. Perhaps the fault was partly their own in the beginning, but, in the main, their condition is forced upon them by their employers. Yet, these degraded people, too, are children of God, and Christ is their brother. There is only one way out, say the militant French Catholics: let authentic Christians share their lives.

Under conditions like these one must listen closely to the Divine Spirit, but, since we are all fallible, it is the community and the team, with the help of the sacerdotal team, which indicates whether the right direction is being followed. It seems a strange apostolate: just to be *present*—sharing such hardships, such sorrows; voluntarily partaking of the everyday life of these forsaken people; enduring the inevitable dirt, the drabness, the inhuman work, the weariness of the body; being completely one of them. Yet, is this not what Christ Himself did?

I could not help remarking to the priest-confessor of a team that, at least, Jesus could contemplate the lovely landscape of Palestine. He had the flowers, the fields and at night the beautiful oriental sky. But the teams? They have a shack outside the factories, no floor, no water, no electricity. They have bedbugs and a filth that no amount of washing could ever clean. They are driven all day long to go faster and faster for wages that do not begin to give them enough to eat.

The priest listened to me thoughtfully and said:

"It may surprise you, but, if there is work to be done, and if the Spirit stirs people up to do it, He also gives them the necessary spiritual means. Perhaps," he added, "it takes women to reach that completeness of abnegation and love."

It would be erroneous to consider this a sentimental, romantic endeavor. It is a "work of the mind," performed with a keen awareness of the state of the world and the imperative necessity for Christians to help all people to come of age and receive their glorious inheritance. The key is friendship. One must "take his neighbor as he is: a sinner and a brother. Do not try to convert him; love him."

A friend of mine once said: "The Party does not want to bother with those people. The Party is convinced that they will benefit automatically from the overthrow of the capitalist regime. But you Christians are interested in restoring everyone, even *those* people. You give your lives for them and probably you will succeed. Their humanity will be awakened. And do you know what will happen? When they are awakened, they will join the Party."

"And is this a good reason why the Christians might as well leave them alone?" I asked.

But later I thought of what a quiet, very fervent priest had told me: "The proletariat's rejection of Christianity is the rejection of its bad representatives, and thereby an adherence to Christianity."

Everywhere the Residents keep in touch with the clergy, especially where there is a sacerdotal team. Some people object to this procedure on the ground that the reason for it, in spite of what has been said, is to make church-goers. This objection is perfectly understandable, but it is not valid, because to the priests, too, "The great revelation of Christianity is its incarnation in daily life. . . . Supernatural life is not an outside garment, but a deep transformation of the whole man."

And so it is that men move on from being "friends of Christ" to being "members of Christ." In their desire to live more fully the fraternal life and the communal effort through the oneness of the Father, they come to feel the need of development and sustainment of their inner life and they discover prayer and the means Christ commanded us to use, so well did He know the weakness of the flesh into which He Himself had descended. Just as in the lives of the Jocists, there comes a time when merely human means proves insufficient to the people of the quarter. Because, when people come of age, authentic Christianity is "not a brake, but a lever."

If we are Christians, we can never stop working

that people may have life and have it more abundantly. But it does not mean that we entertain illusions.

"The religious factor occupies very little space in the life of the masses. . . . The proletariat is a pagan people with Christian superstitions. These superstitions are called baptism, first Communion, marriage, last rites. Of course, one would prefer to believe in God than not believe at all, as is the case in fact. But how can one believe? In church one hears always the same records and the same old stories in Canaan jargon. And that Church, where one should at least find a society which would free you from isolation and artificial separations, that Church leaves you apparently with the same solitude and strengthens the watertight compartments with the whole weight of its drapes, its candles and its classes."

So speaks a monk, a missionary to the proletariat in France. And if a priest can so clearly denounce such a situation, what is to be done? Is it not better to forget about Christianity and let the non-Christian ideologies inspire the people, as they have done for the last hundred years, giving birth to heroes and martyrs? Did not all those of whom I spoke in the first chapter, who suffered persecution for justice's sake, "who believed in heaven and those who did not believe," say that "there was no greater love than to give one's life for a friend?" True. But very few reach that level, whether Christians or non-Christians. Yet, if we think back through the centuries, there has been an imposing number of Christians who have done so. But the great mass of people—and they, not the elite, interest the Christians—"aspire only to change the material conditions of life, to break the determinism which oppresses them in order to take their turn at being its beneficiaries."

That attitude of the masses toward the material aspects of life is extremely important to the Christian, even to the one who prays by word and deed that "Thy will be done on earth as it is in heaven," because the Christian knows that there is no lasting happiness in such an attitude. Why speak of *lasting* happiness? Let us just have happiness for a while, at least, they say. And the Christian says: "We want you to have all the things you should have, physically, materially, intellectually *and* spiritually. You cannot do without that 'spiritually' without being frustrated, cheated and dwarfed into serving a man, a state or a party, instead of the Father." And though, indeed, there is no apparent inclination among the masses at large toward the spiritual, yet the Christian believes that nothing will fill the vacuum in the heart of the masses except God. But "the apostles who go, bringing the Gospel, should truly be able to fill that vacuum."

That imperious necessity has been recognized by many members of the French clergy, and I shall speak later of that tremendous, dynamic and intelligent effort.

It is evident that it is not merely a matter of virtue. A priest can be saintly, but perfectly inadequate for life in the midst of a factory population. Vocations differ. Not everyone is "truly able to fill the vacuum."

In the town we described earlier there are those who are able to do so. They constitute the third panel of the tryptic of the teams. The bishop has given them a parish. Of them and of their work I shall speak in the next chapter. It is sufficient to say here that the sacerdotal team moves along the line of dynamic and communal Christianity.

Through the team of structure and the team of residents we have seen that lay people play an important part in the Christian renewal in France. But they do it in great variety of ways. I wish I had stayed into the spring to "go on a mission." It is an audacious, lively, communal affair. Girls, boys, young married couples, students, scouts, Jocists "invade" a town in a group during Holy Week. None of the young missionaries comes from the town selected. They board with the militants of the town, participate in the local life, meet and talk with the people. Sometimes the first reaction is like the one reported in the newspaper, *Témoignage Chrétien*: "Leave that to the priest," or "Are you going to enter a convent? Or a seminary?"

But the young "missionaries" live their Christian way, and soon the people take to them, because they are young and because it is so obvious that they believe in their Christian mission. They play games with the children, they visit the old and the sick. They give mystery plays.

On Good Friday, after sundown, every group in every quarter of the town gathers behind a cross bearer and they make the Way of the Cross through the town with torches. The groups do eleven stations separately, and at the twelfth they all come together in front of the church. It is deeply impressive. Hundreds of town people follow them. It is one of those mass demonstrations which meet so well the need of our time.

When the young "missionaries" leave town to go back to their own occupations, the people are at the station to see them off. Bonds of friendship have been established. "Come back!" they say. "Next year we, too, want to go on a mission!" A dynamic, fraternal spirit has been awakened: Christ's spirit.

I have shown how a good many French Christians live their Christianity among the proletariat. Some of their ventures may seem daring, but we are in the atomic age, and eighteenth-century manners are out of place. "Christians must become scandalous," the French people say. "They have to be ready to compromise themselves up to the very end." After all, they offer the common man infinitely more than can any political party.

As Léon Bloy says: "It is to start right now to be a

partaker in the Divinity, to be a child of God. *Right now, and* through all eternity, continually rising upward, more and more moving, more impetuous, more and more thunderous, not *toward* God, but *in* God, in the very Essence of the Uncircumscribed."

But to offer that, Christians must understand with Abbé Depierre, "that one is of the Catholic Church only if one is first of humanity, because the body of Christ is the whole humanity, living by His life."

The Workers' Church

ALL OVER THE WORLD, SO-
ciologists and architects have rediscovered the importance of the neighborhood unit. One of those units had
been, for centuries, the parish. To use it, with its
church, is both traditional and extremely modern.

But how use it? To find out, I called at the rectory.
Like all the houses around it, it was dilapidated. The
door was ajar and I went in. I found myself in what
might have been a poor worker's dining room. It was
very poor and drab, because there has been no soap in
France and no paint. There was an old sofa, past repair.
I heard a heavy footstep, and then the door of the dining
room was pushed open and a finely built young workman came in. He was just like any young French
worker, with a turtle-neck sweater and patched pants.
But no, he was not *quite* like any young French worker,

because when I saw his eyes, I knew at once that I should say "Father."

I introduced myself and we shook hands, but he stood there, rather annoyed, and said brusquely: "Look, I'm a factory worker, I'm tired, I was just getting a little sleep before going back to work. That's what I am: a worker, and I *don't* like talking."

I understood. There is nothing the French dislike more, when they are really doing something, than publicity. But I explained to him that I was not concerned with publicity stunts, or with him as an individual. I was concerned with learning the truth about France and French Christianity. So he sat on the old sofa and we talked. Other members of the team came in. It was toward the end of the day and they were all very tired, but there was a light in their eyes. There was an utter simplicity about them, an earnestness and serene fervor. I felt as if I could not ask any more questions, but I remember saying, "Who cooks for you?" I think that at the time it was the only thing I wanted to do: not ask questions, but cook for them.

Of the five on the team, two were regular priests and three secular. Even this was a novelty. There is a belief among the workers that the regular and secular clergy do not get along together. Yet here they were, working side by side, no one knowing who was pastor— just a team. Living in the rectory was only temporary.

Three of them had just found rooms with workers' families.

The two Dominicans had found boards with which to build a shack among the shacks of the poorest people. Before living at the rectory, one had received permission to leave off his habit and work as a longshoreman among the waterfront toughs. At first he went home to the monastery at night. But he soon realized that the longshoreman would never feel that he was one of them if he did not live among them. He was permitted to make the change, and I do not know of any more dynamic, straightforward, unsentimental and deeply human a narrative than the account of his new life. There was picturesqueness and pathos and stark tragedy in what he told, yet he managed never to lose sight of his broad objective.

While I was at the rectory, a man popped his head inside the door and said to the priest-worker who was talking to me: "Hey, Jacques, come out a minute please. Old mother 'X' wants to talk to you." And "Jacques" went out. That is the way. Some men call them by their first name and use the familiar "thou," the women say "Father" or "Father Jacques" or, for the Dominicans, "White Father." Willingness to accept the sacerdotal team is due to the removal of all barriers. First, there was the barrier of celibacy. The idea had been that it was all a "put-up job," and that the priests were not really faithful to their vows. But when they actually lived and worked in the same quarters day and night, the men had to recognize the truth. Moreover, the workers understand readily that, in order to give oneself to a cause, one cannot marry. Even the communist party advises its leaders not to marry. So that was easy.

But the main difficulty was the money question. So the team's first move was to eliminate seating arrangements by financial status in the churches, and to abolish fixed fees for ceremonies. There were no more collections. A box was placed at the entrance of the church where people could put what they wanted. This was all a move in the right direction.* But for centuries there had been so much "noise of silver" around the altar that the workers were only half satisfied. True, the church had ceased to be an administrative organization, and the priests were no longer mere functionaries of birth, marriage and death. But many people still said that the priests were living on what the workers gave them. It seemed, then, to the team, as it did to others that in order to break down prejudices, rehabilitate manual work (Christ Himself had done manual work) and redeem the Church in the eyes of the workingman, the only thing to do was for the priests to make their own living by manual labor.

* It must be understood that whatever is done in France by the clergy, regular and secular, is, of course, never done in opposition to the hierarchy.

They are doing it. A definite *modus vivendi* has not yet been established, but the priests who are doing manual work will do so for the rest of their lives. The attitude of the population has changed. Sneers are gone, friendly respect has entered, and a sort of wonder: "What manner of men are these?" They seem like anyone else. They stand in line after working hours to get their groceries, fill their pails of water at the tap in the courtyard, empty their garbage cans, chase the inevitable bedbugs and use the common toilet. Whatever they have, they are always ready to share. And, being workers, they work for the elimination of the proletariat, shoulder to shoulder with the team of structures and the team of residents. And they have something else to offer, the thing which is like a lightning flash, the one reality which can fill the vacuum. Steadily, surely, the Church of the workers is being built.

It is all new to this particular town; discoveries are being made every day. In the parish church there was a baptism, and, as one of the godfathers explained to me: "It was in such familiar language! And it was so beautiful! We, how could we know? Before, we never understood anything. At the end, Father said: 'Go in peace, my little Michel.' And he kissed him. And a real kiss, not a priest's kiss."

At a wedding the couple kissed at the foot of the altar: "It was all so simple and so engaging." And at funerals the priests explain everything, and they don't go around telling you that "everything is all right." They take time to grieve with you, and, when they speak of hope, you don't mind listening, because it is as if they really shared your sorrow. The whole thing is like a big family, and the people respond. As for the priests, they say: "The thing to do is to humanize the sacraments." Instead of seeming like automatic distributors of "favors" which can be paid for, so that the sacraments have come to be mere superstition or magic to the common man, let the clergy be more faithful to the teaching of the Church and make the people *feel the need* of the sacraments and receive them with an ever-increasing joy of fulfillment. And so the parish church in this town is becoming the Church of the workers, their own assembly.

It is not because I think "the proletariat is an end in itself," as Mauriac would put it, that I am specially concerned with it, but because the whole world is thinking about the workers at this time. Some people think of them with dread, and some with clenched fists. It is all very grim, whether it is fear or violence. But wherever I have been with the teams and with the workers who surround them, Christians and non-Christians, I have found a seriousness which does not exclude gaiety, a bold determination without hatred, and a facing of facts which acted as a springboard for the infinite possibilities of man as a child of God.

It has been a long time in France since one has seen a white-robed Dominican talking with men in the street. People bring chairs out to the sidewalk, and passersby stop to listen. Who has ever seen a priest discussing the Gospel with other men in the cafés? "The workers have been invited to come and hear about the Gospel in the places which are more accessible to them, each man giving his own point of view. The conversations have been direct and above board. The communists were in the majority." So reads the local newspapers in a French town.

And who has seen a team going down into the mines as workmen? Two priest-miners were talking to me. One was the son of a railroad worker; the other, a mining engineer. The third I did not meet. None of the three had been ordained as yet, but all had worked in the mines for several months. They had received their vocations through their devotion to Charles de Foucauld. The simplicity and strength of their testimony, the maturity of their outlook, their up-to-date competence and their virile thinking make them outstanding human beings. And, in addition, there is the fervent total offering of themselves. They admit that the project they have started on is pure folly in human eyes. They think that it will take them perhaps thirty years to become competent miners—like the thirty years at Nazareth. They do not contemplate any apostolate, apart from sharing the common destiny of the miners, their work, dangers, sorrows and joys, sharing them with the intensity and clear insight which their Christian priesthood gives them.

The team holds all material things in common. In 1946 they rented a small miner's cottage. The three lived there together, pooling everything and keeping open house while above ground. Soon, the people were interested, having seen their communal way of life and their readiness to share and lend anything as neighbors. Borrowed money was always returned. They took in a young miner. Soon he was perfectly at home. He used to watch them quietly while they prayed and read the Breviary and the Bible.

By the time the three left, they had made many friends. They long to go back. They said to me: "The mine is our fiancée. We are separated from her just now. But the day of our ordination will be our wedding day." They are no dreamers. They are husky fellows, matter-of-fact and keen of mind. And they are going into the pits for the rest of their lives to bring love, the only deliverer—that which, they say, communism ignores.

Miles away from there, in a large factory town, I knocked at the door of a poor worker's house. A blond, healthy young giant opened the door. He wore a khaki shirt and worker's pants.

"Father 'X'?"

"Yes."

The room was small. There was a little iron bed. A round table stood in the middle. An iron pot sat on a tiny round stove. Photos and pictures hung on the wall. On the table lay a large crucifix and a portable altar. On the little iron bed were spread an alb and chasuble.

"I bet you haven't eaten. You will have supper with us, won't you?" Father "X" had discerned at once that I was not there out of curiosity, and I thanked him inwardly.

The door opened, and Father "T" came in from another factory, looking like a spent young workman at the end of the day. He went up to his room. As usual, the team lived together and had everything in common. By the time he came back we had set the table and put on the soup. I had discovered the kitchen, which was a grotto of stalactites when the gas stove was not lighted.

Father "X" spoke of the Mass he had celebrated when he came back from the factory. He had been dressing there in his room and thinking that since no one was coming he might not be able to celebrate, when the door opened and a boy came in. He asked whether Father would go and visit an old sick lady in one of the tenements. And Father "X" said: "Why, of course! And why not celebrate Mass there?"

The boy's eyes widened and he said: "But you can't do that. It isn't done!"

"And who told you so? You'll see." And the boy ran ahead to announce the news. The neighbors cleaned the room and set it in order. Father "X" put everything necessary in his bag and went. Of course, the old woman nearly died of joy. All the neighbors came, crowding into the room, spilling over into the hall, standing out on the stairway. It was a wonderful Mass. When he was leaving, some workers asked if he could not do the same at their home another time. Christ had been brought suddenly nearer to them than He had ever been before, and they were surprised, and proud.

Here I was told, as I had been told before, how necessary it was that the working class should be made to rediscover the sacraments through their need of them. I was told that the first step toward a reawakening of spiritual life is friendship, communal Christianity.

While we were eating, the neighbors, men and women, came and went, seeking advice, a chat, a piece of news. When supper was over we sang a joyful song of thanksgiving and washed the dishes. Father "X" quoted a fellow worker at the factory: "So, you're a priest, and you're going to be a factory worker? For how long? A year? Two? Five? Ten?"

"Why, for the rest of my life."

"Well, pal, if you stick it out until the workers' pension, I'll believe."

Let me add an account of what was happening in the industrial suburb of another large town. We crossed a yard and opened a door into a workman's house. About twenty people, more men than women, were in the kitchen. Steam from the pots on the gas stove gave the room its only warmth. I knew only one person, but soon we were all talking to one another. It was seven o'clock, after working hours. Father "N" came in. He had the build of a young peasant (which he was) and the cordiality of a factory worker (which he also was). He wore a dark brown suit and a vivid blue muffler, clothes that had been given to him. But if, the next day, he were to find someone in dire need, he might doff everything, even his shoes, and again put on overalls and string-sole shoes. One would never look for him to be dressed in the same outfit from day to day. After he had shaken hands all around, he went to a room off the kitchen. After a while he opened the door and we all went in, except a communist friend who was going to watch the cooking while Mass was celebrated.

It was a small, drab room. Father "N" had vested himself. We stood in a semi-circle around the table and

Father "N" faced us. We all responded in French, following the Mass in little booklets. During the Canon we answered in Latin. He read the Gospel of the day; then quietly asked, "What do you think of it?" We talked it over familiarly, Father "N" never using a stereotyped answer, but speaking with straightforwardness and earnestly seeking to clarify. At the Offertory, a man went around with a little box full of wafers. Those who were to receive Communion would take one of the wafers, go to the table and put it on the paten which Father "N" was holding. The Mementos were said aloud in French and anyone who wished could name specific persons. At the Memento of the Living, a sick neighbor was mentioned; Father "N" named the communist comrade who was watching our supper, and I some American Catholic friends. The same was done at the Memento of the Dead. We were all very near: the living we knew and loved, and the dear ones passed away. Kneeling on the floor, we received Communion.

"*Ite, missa est.*" Father "N" was radiant of face. "How about singing a song?"

He started a song written by the popular French composer, Bouchor, on the theme of the Ninth Symphony. I am afraid that song was mostly men's work! At least, they took the lead. While Father "N" removed his vestments, we went back to the kitchen. Our communist friend had everything under control.

The men arranged the small tables to make one big one, and everyone helped set out the plates, knives, forks and glass. We sat anywhere and on anything.

It was all very gay. Stories were told, and I think Father "N" had the best ones. But I am sure he regretted asking me to tell them something about America. "Yes! Yes!" demanded the group. "Well," I said, "shoot the questions, and I shall try to answer." It was not exactly prudent. We spent nearly the whole evening. There was one young man, especially, who was full of questions. It was a relief when Father "N" finally put an end to the session by saying good-humoredly, "That young one is determined to learn everything before morning!"

Neighbors had come in during the evening. We found room for them and went on talking and eating. How, one might ask, can there be enough to eat in a place where there seem to be no contributions and all the people are poor? But everyone brings something, and sometimes the ingredients of these quasi-impromptu meals are quite startling. Most of us left around eleven o'clock. Father's day was not yet finished, for people still were coming to see him.

I came out with a sense of deep joy and a feeling of oneness with all who were there. That assembly, that *ecclesia,* that Church in the back kitchen, might be called a mission church. But the parish church of which I spoke earlier is also a mission. In any case, the people have ceased identifying Church and bourgeoisie.

Around Father "N" many neighborly communities and activities have started. Here, as in many other places, the communists find themselves outdistanced by the Christians.

Father "N" knows of ten young workmen who want to become priest-workers, but he tells them: "Wait. In order to be a priest one should be a man first and have suffered the sufferings of men. To be called 'Father' is not for nothing. You will have to be that, not only to children but to men, too, especially to men as a priest-worker. So wait." He says that he is young himself and knows that young enthusiasm does not always last. He probably is also wary of the excessive zeal of new converts. Further, he has a keen sense of the burdens the world puts on the shoulders of the priest. Finally, he knows that the Seminary of the Mission of France, of which I shall speak later, is full to overflowing. But the factory workers who yesterday were atheists and today are considering the priesthood are big news, because it means they did not meet "a clergyman, but a man of God." And that is what is happening in many places in France.

It is easy to see that the kindling of the spirit of Christ among the workers is found in a variety of styles in France just now. The whole thing is bubbling up here and there, all over, and keeps the hierarchy busy. No sooner have they, after due consideration, given their approval to this or that request, than laymen and clergy pop up with something else to decide upon. There are great men in the French hierarchy, men of outstanding intelligence, whose far-sighted audacity is joined with a steadfast grip to the authentic tradition of the Church. Without their understanding and their integral Catholicism, nothing could be accomplished.

If they can hardly keep up with all that is happening, it is clear that I cannot even begin to make a thorough survey. I can only mention landmarks which I found here and there. It is very difficult to keep the issues separate, which I must do as a convenience in discussion. The issues are often interlocked, as in the case of workers' churches and parish churches. There are really no such divisions. Where the kindling of the spirit of Christ is concerned, it is the whole thing which starts moving: all the people—non-Christians, lay Christians, clergy—and, therefore, communal expression. It is impossible to regard the things that are afoot in France as things to be studied, explained and neatly disposed of in compartments of the mind. The Christian movement just *is*. It discourages analysis and eludes the reporting sense, because it is not matter for publicity.

This is so much the case that many French people, even members of the clergy, know little or nothing about the extent of the movement I am trying to record in this book. I remember a distinguished Benedictine who was doing great things for the renewal. I was telling him some of what I had seen in other parts of France. "Will the book be published in French?" he asked. "All of us don't know what the others are doing and how much is being done, and we want to know."

The Peasants' Church

FORTY-FIVE PERCENT OF THE
French population belongs to the peasant class. Going
about France, seeing the processions, the attendance at
Mass, the baptisms, the first Communions, the weddings
and the funerals, one might be tempted to conclude
that de-Christianization has not been felt in the country. But, if one talks to the people or to any country
priest, one makes these discoveries, as has Abbé Boulard:

"The peasant religion is a religion of fear, consist-
ing of interdictions. It is as if God forbade happiness."

"Religion is judged by acts of piety, not by professional duties or charity."

"Religion is not truly personal and has become
conformist. The importance of 'what is done' and 'what
is not done' is extreme."

"The peasants' religion is individualistic, one might
say selfish."

"My Christians . . . consider God a faraway God, to whom one should submit as much as possible, not out of love of Him, but out of fear of going to hell. God is not the Father; Christ is not the Brother who unites us to the Father. No. God is the one who set down the ten negative commandments: 'Thou shalt not . . .' Christ is not much known. Grace is a happy passing state which one should manage to be in at the time of death in order not to go to hell. . . . Conclusion: God stands in the way of happiness; therefore, He is of little attraction to the young people when an ideal or passion urges them."

It is easy to see that such loveless "Christianity" ends in a ritualistic religion, only a few steps from superstition or complete indifference. In either case there is de-Christianization, that is to say, no Christianity of life. Often, the process runs like this: Parents have only a ritualistic religion colored with superstition. Children, when they grow up, hasten to escape from the coercion of a religion which consists more in keeping one's accounts square with God than in being "alive in Him."

As in the case of city workers, it is not a matter of making church-goers of the country people, or even of increasing their number, since, generally speaking, church attendance is much better than in the cities. The problem is to recapture the spirit of Christ and have the communities live by it.

Just as there is a youth movement in the cities, the JOC, there is one in the country, the JAC (Jeunesse Agricole Catholique). It has evolved since the war into an all-inclusive movement, radiating through the whole life of the community.

An athletic young peasant member of the JAC to whom I spoke said, in substance: "We do not go in for an apostolate. We are up against the usual rural idea that Christians do not like progress, and we labor to raise the professional level of the peasant. Country people think that Christians are not gay, and we busy ourselves having fun during leisure time. The starting point for the Christian life is to do something together, whether the people are formally interested in the JAC or not."

Professionally, or during leisure time, the people work for the good of others. Professionally, much is being done. Young people are encouraged to take courses in scientific exploitation, new techniques, psychology. They are encouraged to participate actively in the rural unions. The JAC favors any union initiative which truly assists the farmer. But, of course, the JAC stands firm against making an idol of any professional organization. It is particularly against any reform handed down from higher up. In the question of tractors, for instance, it favors communal, neighborly grouping to procure them, whereas the communists advocate enormous centers of tractors handed down from a central source. The JAC system is harder to establish, because it requires an active participation *from the bottom up,* and people too often prefer reforms to be handed down, even if it means a lessening of their humanity. But that is precisely where authentic Christianity is leaven in the dough and prevents a civilization from sinking to low levels.

The use of leisure time is also carefully considered, not, as a priest remarked, because "it makes better people of those who are helped, but because it kindles the charity of Christ within those who help." It is through their souls that a renewed Christianity can reach the souls of their brothers. Yet, we are reminded by Abbé Boulard that "Generous souls, or souls that will become generous, must sometimes be looked for, not among the serious young, but among the devil-may-cares at a bar, to whom the population listens."

A great effort is being made to awaken the creative spirit through evening gatherings at the farms, where people tell stories, sing, play games and work for festivals connected with the soil. There are still very few cars in France, and driving to the nearest motion-picture theater to spend a passive evening is problematical. Nevertheless, there is no negative attitude toward the movies when they can be seen, or the radio when it can be heard. The slogan is to "see, judge and do something." As for the interchange of ideas at the evening gatherings, my young peasant friend mentioned that there was little conversation. Unlike the young city people, the country youth could not be induced to talk on religion or love. They considered it in bad taste.

A Christian community should radiate its thoughts and ideals. The country newspaper, *Jeunes Forces Rurales,* says: "It is not enough to make a *success* of your life. You should make a *gift* of it. You must be a giver of life, the life of the soul and the life of the body, the material and the spiritual. Do not be only a consumer in the Church, but also a producer."

The JAC initiates "permanent campaigns of fraternity." Anyone who knows the sterling value of the French peasant, as well as his proverbial avariciousness, will realize that the JAC could hardly have hit on a more difficult approach. But it is the only approach that will touch the core of the situation. So the peasant community helps a worker community; it sends vegetables and food packages from the country. It will adopt a city family or act as godmother to the sick in the sanataria. During the war, villages which had not been bombed "adopted" other villages which had been wiped out.

The young militants operate on a team-work basis. Packages are made up of food which they have set aside from their own personal rations. When one considers that ration tickets in France do not provide nearly enough for the people to feed themselves adequately, it becomes apparent that, when the militants set aside food out of their personal allowances, they are virtually giving of their own substance. It is true, of course, that in the country there are foods that do not exist in the city. That is why "permanent campaigns of fraternity" could be started in the first place. Nevertheless, there are things which the country does not provide at all, such as sugar, coffee (*ersatz*, of course!), chocolate and oranges. In any event, the militants have to start the campaign by giving their own share of food, whether rationed or not. They first have to persuade their own parents to let them take vegetables from the garden or put aside, every day, their own egg or share of butter. It takes time, faith and determination to make up those first packages. But, soon the village knows about it and is curious, if not sympathetic.

The day the packages are brought to the post office there is talk all around, and much criticism: "People shouldn't put their noses into other people's business." There are bitter words from the parents: "Do you think I have slaved to bring you up, just to see you wasting away for the sake of good-for-nothing city people?" But it has been brought home to the village, for the first time, that some people are starving. Some people *are* starving. And these young people are feeding them.

Their elders, of course, insist it is all foolishness. Is it for others that one works so hard on the farm? And yet, very very slowly, the village takes to the idea. The young "apostles" make the rounds of the village.

"At 'L,' where the rounds are made monthly, there is an old lady who has always refused to give anything. What can be done about it? In the garden the militants see some beautiful parsley. 'Madame, it's for the package for the worker family in the city. In town one cannot find any parsley, and yours is so beautiful. . . .' Now, every month, the old lady adds six leeks to the parsley. At 'R' the owner of the grocery store does not want to give anything. But she is prevailed upon for paper and string! And now, each month, she gets it ready in advance."

In order to make cakes at Christmas time for the city children, the militants make the rounds. "Please, madame, one tablespoon of flour." It is impossible to refuse one tablespoonful of flour, even when the flour is rationed. But here is a family so poor that they cannot even do that. So the militants ask for "a pinch of salt." It is given gladly, and a few precious lumps of sugar are added.

"There was a village near an industrial town," reports Boulard, from whom several of these accounts were taken, "where it seemed impossible to open the hearts of the people to the misery of the city. Every-

thing had been tried: packages, rounds, adoptions. . . .
The militants were not discouraged. They waited.
Every Saturday some workers went through to try and
collect some food farther on. One winter day a worker
was found in the village street, dead from cold and lack
of food. The village was very upset. Without losing a
minute, the militants made the most of the tragedy.
The young men were corralled to build a shack on the
road. The women managed to collect stove and pans.
A round was made for vegetables. The girls made soup.
All winter, every Saturday and Sunday, the factory
workers could stop there, warm themselves and have
hot soup. When summer came, the village, which had
opened up its heart through this first gesture, decided
to adopt in a group all the children of the neighbor-
ing industrial town."

Of course all this accomplishment is not an end in
itself, but a channel for the flow of divine life. The
community is aroused to do something for distant
brothers. Soon many young people decide to become
militants: "If religion is *doing* something . . ." they
say, "well . . ." There are, of course, two dangers.
First, people might come to think that social action *is*
religion. But the militants are well aware of this, and
they make it clear to others that, while social action is
not religion, yet religion, Christ, must be incarnated in
social action as He must be in all things human, each one

of us bearing Christ's spirit everywhere into temporal affairs. The second danger is that people might come to think that it is sufficient to help others spontaneously without bothering about what can be done to remedy the general bad distribution. The Christian militants combat this conception by refusing to detach themselves from temporal concerns (as so many have done during the last century especially, in spite of all the papal injunctions).

There is a Christian way of organizing adequate distribution of the goods of this earth, and some of the Christians who take part in the "campaigns of fraternity" study distribution and other economic problems; they work within existing organisms and create new ones along fraternal lines. Whether they work through professional improvements, leisure activities or campaigns of fraternity, all participants work jointly. It is a true communal effort. As Abbé Boulard says:

"We must gather these Christians into communities, as well as the men and women who try to become Christians. For it is to the *communal* testimony that Christ particularly promised the convincing sign of His presence. . . . It was the firm practice of the early Church to bear testimony to Christ through the radiating strength of lively and united communities. . . . The same testimony is, today, still irresistible— Christ's promise is there—and indispenable."

The French Catholics insist upon it. The effort is not toward "making church-goers or toward the 'salvation' of each individual, or the foundation of a new Christianity. To make Christians, and *authentic* Christians, is to make each individual *conscious of his duty of charity toward God and his brothers,* and then to help him, through the practice of sacraments. Life in a Christian community means to fulfil that duty completely."

Communists smile: "It's all poppycock. No worthwhile change can be accomplished without the overthrow of capitalism." Suppose that the hardness of the capitalists' hearts and their shortsightedness justify the communists' affirmation, does it mean that all Christians have to become Marxists in order to bring effectively more of Christ's spirit on this earth? Our disagreement with communism is not over the sharing of material goods. From the Fathers of the Church up to the present time the Church has taught that material goods should be shared by all and not piled up for the profit of a few individuals. No, our disagreement is basic. We cannot be Marxists because "we believe." What possibly can be the inducement of Marxism to people who believe to the letter that when Jesus told his disciples to say "Our Father" to God he really meant it?

Other objections might well be raised. First, about being conscious of the duty of "charity." It is an abused word. But I heard a priest—a factory-worker—explain it: "If I have two shirts, and the man I know does not have any, my second shirt belongs to him. It is not a gift I am making him. In a Christian sense the second shirt belongs to him. That's what charity means."

Then, what about the full practice of the sacraments? It would seem that the fraternal country people do go to church after all, though declarations are thrown to the four winds that "the aim of the Christian effort is not to make church-goers." And if that is so, where do the priests come into the picture?

Let us first consider the priest as he fits into the rural picture of France. Country priests in France have always had a remarkable devotion to their calling, and, in a country where there are few cars, they have suffered bitterly from isolation. An effort is now being made to end their solitude. Again, it is along the communal line. What is true of the faithful is true of the hierarchy. And what is true of the material life is true of the spiritual life. One cannot (generally speaking, though there have been notable individual exceptions) recharge the batteries of spiritual life alone. The tragic life of Bernanos' country priest is familiar to many readers. The communion of the living is a necessity and a reality, a premise of the communion of saints.

In our age, especially, it is most necessary that people gather together frequently, not only to talk things over, but to pray together, live together and have fun together. This is being attempted in different ways. One method is to make a center of the pastor's residence, where priests from scattered villages meet weekly. This arrangement satisfies the inclination of priests who prefer not to follow the conventual life, precisely because they cannot accept full communal existence. At the same time it prevents all from slipping into a private world; it provides a spiritual "refilling station."

The pastor helps the priests co-ordinate their efforts. They divide their territorial field according to their own natural abilities and the exigencies of a live Christianity. Some are most fitted for preaching; some have a knack for working with young people; some are best in the confessional. The preachers can go out and preach, and the others work with young people or make the round for confessions. This does not mean that the resident will give up preaching or meeting the young or hearing confession. But it does mean freshness and expansion for the clergy and lay people.

Unfortunately, there are too many places in the country where there are no priests at all, and the people are left alone. The story is told of one village whose communist mayor went to the bishop and asked him for a priest.

"But why do *you* ask for a priest?" said the bishop.

"Well," replied the mayor, "a priest is so decorative in a village."

He *is* decorative. He belongs to the landscape. He does fit in the picture. A village without a priest has lost a fundamental figure. The communist mayor felt it. His village was not complete. Of course, the question is: What lies behind that loss? Some men and women feel it keenly and are taking over. Jacists living in priestless villages ring the bell for the evening Angelus, and gather together in an empty church to recite Complines. The village people are joining in, and spiritual concern is awakening.

But the Jacists, fervent as they are, are not enough. To help the endeavor, Country Missionary Brothers, some of whom are priests, some laymen, go into the priestless countryside and preach the Gospel. The Country Dominicans, a new feminine order, functions in places too far from any center for the people to go to church. They labor among their forsaken populations without having, themselves, the help of Communion. These conditions would be familiar to many pioneer Sisters in America, except that the absence of cars, and even the impossibility in many steep places of using a bicycle, make the loneliness more complete in France. Jacists, priests, missionaries, Sisters do not want to leave people anywhere alone with their difficulties and their sorrows, but to share them.

Let us now consider the question of the sacraments.

This chapter has so far concerned the awakening of the dynamic fraternal and communal spirit in France and the reader might well wonder where the sacraments come in. One might even ask me to justify the expression, "peasant *church*." I recall what a young French coal miner said to me when I spoke about a well-known American film about Catholicism which I had admired. The young miner annihilated me when he queried: "What do they think the Church is over there? A building?"

The reader knows better. Ever since the beginning of Christianity, whenever Christians have met for the purpose of worship, they have done certain things. To the Catholic, the sacraments are an indissoluble part of Christian life. It may seem, from all I have said, that French Christians are bent on fraternal and communal effort without any religious "practice." Unfortunately, there has been too much dead "practice." Practice is not to be done away with, of course, nor is it to be fundamentally changed, but it has to be rediscovered before it is followed. This requires patience and understanding from the priest who lives among the people. If he lacks these qualities, all can be lost. As my peasant friend remarked: "Sometimes we still have difficulties with the old clergy who cling to the notion of the priest as the "boss," and sometimes we have trouble with overzealous chaplains who rush the newly awakened through the sacraments."

To stand by and wait until the people want to talk with a priest and feel the need of the sacraments calls for a new expression of love, but does not mean that the sterling virtues of the French clergy have been rejected, least of all does it mean that the teaching of the Church has been tampered with. But it does mean that the relationship between priest and people is in need of a new approach. As a priest puts it: "Today, life demands more initiative of thought and action of the Christians who want to have influence. Therefore, the role of the priest is to *help them to come of age,* to teach them to do without him in what is their own responsibility."

My peasant friend remarked that many Jacists, not feeling the *need* of the sacraments, remain away from Church for years. The impact of the fraternal message of Christianity strikes them first—sacramental life comes later. A young farmer has this to say:

"I had understood part of Christianity. At a meeting of the sector a list of questions on the Gospel which dealt with love for one's neighbor had been truly a revelation to me. But I was far from understanding it all. I understood no better than before the liturgical and sacramental life, and, as I wished to be logical with myself, I did not want to do anything more that did not make sense to me."

It may seem strange to some Catholics who link the Church with authoritarianism to hear of a country—known as the eldest Daughter of the Church—with such absence of coercion. But the Church in France has always been able to discriminate between pride and integrity of mind. And she knows that the exacting mind of the French people—be they intellectuals, factory workers or peasants—is a God-given gift, which is to be highly respected and helped, and not crushed.

How long the country population will remain in this intermediary Christian stage is a question the Catholic workers do not ask themselves. They trust the power of the Spirit, and they know from experience that at first the ways of grace are often disconcerting. They labor, pray, partake of the Holy Eucharist themselves and leave the rest to God. Whenever the "new" Christians come to use the sacraments, it is because they feel the need of them and desire them, and wish to bring Christ—whose boundless fraternal message they have so readily grasped—more fully to the community.

CHAPTER SEVEN

The Parish

THE PARISH ORIGINATED IN the first centuries of the Christian era with the grouping together of Christians under the direction of a leader who was Christ's representative. Gradually, the community organized its life according to its Jewish heritage and its own needs: meetings for prayer and religious instruction, eucharistic and disciplinary assemblies, social assistance assemblies. The parish was a natural, popular outgrowth of the synagogue. Lay participation was very great, for the parish was the people; it was not an agglomeration, but a group living in a certain place under the direction of an Apostle or apostolic successor. Community life was the parish. There were identity and unity: so very much so that, when the people of France felt, in the thirteenth century, that they must assert their rights against the lords, grants were made communally. The commune was one with the parish. The church was the center of the parish and was, therefore, the center of the community. The parish was a territorial unit. Now, however, the parish merely comprises those who go to church in a particular building.

There was a time when all the people, men especially, whether peasants or workers, were at home in the parish church. But for a long time now it has been only the home of the bourgeois. Some, of course, will hasten to say that it is so because the people have liberated themselves from the Church. But we who believe that Christianity has within itself the germs of the greatest possible development that the intelligence of man may ever come to desire cannot sit back and accept defeat. However, we should recognize that, if a divorce has taken place, it is because countless Christians have failed to fulfill their brothers' spiritual and material needs. The French parish has ceased to be an expression of communal life. As Abbé Michonneau has said:

"Either the parish will remain closed up in the 'parochial group,' and the world of the people will remain outside, or else the parish will open up itself as a 'community.' In the latter case there will be a crisis. There will be tensions, difficulties, protestations from the deadweights and the followers of routine. But, if St. Paul wins, the world of the people will accede to Christianity."

Christ was of the people. He was followed by the people, and His message was, and still is, for the people. And the people take to it easily, but "what throws them off is the way we present it."

Recently in France a number of people belonging to the hard physical trades, such as the *forts des Halles*, have become Christians. They have great virile fervor and attend Mass in back kitchens, as I have described. They feel they are a part of it; they are at home and, at the same time, full of reverence and joy. One day, a group of these men entered a regular parish church during Mass. They stayed to the end and waited. Then, puzzled, they went home. The next time they saw the priest who had been the instrument of their conversion they said to him placidly: "We went to such and such church, but there were no Christians there." The priest just looked at them, thinking that they were trying to be clever. But they were in complete earnest, utterly unconscious of any incongruity in their remark. "No," they went on. "We kept asking the people around us when the Christians were going to have their meeting. They just laughed at us. These people had come to see a spectacle and did not know about the Christians. We kept wondering how long the spectacle would last, but it went on and on. Then they passed a plate. We didn't give anything, of course, because we had not come to see a spectacle. When it was finally over, we waited for the Christians, but everyone left. We left, too, guessing that it was the wrong time for the meeting of the Christians."

The church where the workers had attended high Mass was inadequate because it had lost its link with the people. The French workers and the rest of the people who have not adopted a bourgeois style of living or thinking are no longer at home in most of the parish churches.

This is not to say that the bourgeois should feel at home in the parish church. The fact is that those bourgeois who still have a spark of life are groping for a renewal of parish life. They are finding expression in actively participating in the liturgy. I was amazed to find a bourgeois church where the people actually seemed to have rediscovered Christianity—a stark, unsentimental, burning Christianity. Centuries seemed to have been abolished. Saint Paul was in our midst, as well as St. Stephen and St. Felicity. We did not "think" about them. They were with us, and we with them, in an almost unbearable communion, as we all gathered around the altar which had been brought down near the communion rail: the dining table of Holy Thursday, ageless. The priest faced the people. He pronounced every word distinctly, and all answered distinctly, in full voice. There was directness, virility, cool and heroic concentration. A reader among the faithful arose and read in French the Introit, the Epistle, the Gospel, the Offertory, the Communion and the Post Communion. *"Domine, non sum dignus . . ."* Each of us said it aloud, in his own way, with his whole self, but the fervor blended us all and brought us in one sweep, all together, to the Communion table.

To remake Christians of the bourgeoisie is as great a problem as to achieve it with the manual workers. But there is a difference. If I have chosen to speak especially of the proletariat, it is because they had not too much opportunity to remain Christians during the last few centuries.

We are confronted now by a situation in which those workers who are won over to Christ do not feel at home in His church. Even just before the war, when the JOC for instance, still was "fishing with a line or fishing with a net" for Christians, it became evident that the new converts either adapted themselves to the bourgeois parish church, and consequently, lost their identity with the working class, or else did not adapt themselves at all, and sooner or later ceased being active Christians. Some parishes made the adaptation possible. But, since we are now, more than ever, intent on "changing the water in the pond," the incorporation of a whole new body of men and women is in the making, and the problem is considerable.

Those who have been awakened to the spirit of

Christ say this to us: "You taught us that really to love one's neighbor is to have Christ in one's heart. And now we do love Christ. We would die for Him. But what has that to do with all the stuff that goes on in the parish church, all the mumbling, all the awful old women, the sugar-coated statues, and the words we do not understand?"

We reply: "You are right and you are wrong. These things should not be. You should, above all, understand what is going on. All that you complain of can be changed without endangering the Church's teaching. But you are wrong if you conclude that the parish church is no good at all. Christianity is a communal affair, and the parish church exists. It is a fact. It should be used."

People have to meet together, simply because they want to. On the other hand, it is wise to wait patiently for them to feel the need of the sacraments. They have a passion for living the life of friendship which is Christ's, and sooner or later they are confronted, as we all are, by their own inadequacy. They take nothing for granted, and, being young in their faith and untrammeled by worldly goods, they do not believe that convenient formulas or administrative procedures will straighten everything out. They feel a desperate need to be grafted onto Christ Himself through the Holy Eucharist, to be a member of Christ and to know that others are members of Christ. There may be some, of course, who do not and never will sense the need, and there is little that can be done about it at the moment. The aim of the French Christians is not, after all, to make mere church-goers.

As to those who desire a full Christian life, all is well so long as they assemble at the "mission." But the moment they step into the parish church they feel lost. The lay people and clergy of the parish church must not wash their hands of the situation; to do so means to aggravate the sickness.

I have already pointed out that men and women who have been steeped in church traditions for generations and who, in some cases at least, know its value cannot throw everything overboard because others have not a full understanding of the Church. The parish church has inherited a wealth of spiritual values, which, beyond question, may not be discarded, but should be passed on to new Christians—not, however, as museum pieces, but as *living realities*. Therefore, the movement should be in both directions: the new converts have to learn; the parish church has to renew itself.

The dynamic new converts are very willing to learn, provided that they are not presented with dead routine. We might just as well face the fact: What is to be taught them is often entirely new to the old parishioners themselves, who have slipped into slumber.

The French have found out that they need a rediscovery of the priesthood and the religious apostolate along the lines of Christian communal life.

The parish church should renew itself in spirit first. At the St. Flour Convention of September, 1945, the problem was stated thus:

"A solution has to be found. We are not interested in mere novelties. We are not gathered here together to advocate the dialogue Mass, the altar facing the people, the reading in French of certain passages of the Mass, still less a particular shape of chasuble or dalmatic.

"It is life itself which has to be found: the life of the Church. To find it, it is and always will be necessary to have much intelligence, imagination, heart and, what is even more necessary, the permanent and fertilizing action of the Holy Ghost. We are called upon to make a permanent effort."

As soon as the parish church becomes willing to renew itself in spirit, it finds itself up against a huge question: the question of money. We have seen that, in the missions, the priest-workers and residents have removed that wall of separation. They have set out on the proletarian path of insecurity and, once you do that, it does not matter so much whether you are a manual worker or an intellectual: you share a community of destiny with the proletariat. We have seen, in one parish church, a member of the sacerdotal team working full time in a factory. This set-up, very recently tried, has had favorable consideration from other parish churches anxious to renew themselves, but not able to have every priest working outside.

Even the workers have come to realize that the priest has not the time for his full job as a worker and his full job as a parish priest. There is one "mission" where a priest has been relieved by the hierarchy of all parish duties so that he can spend all his time in a factory. He has made many friends, and many workers have come to Christ through him. Christian communities have sprung up all around the neighborhood.

But one day the workers said to him: "Look, you can't go on like this. You have to quit the factory and just be our priest. When we elect a mayor, he has to quit his job if he is a factory worker. Well, we have chosen you to be our priest, so you have to quit. We need you."

The workers understand that to be a priest is to hold a job. But they can understand it only as long as the priest is as insecure as they are.

And how can they feel otherwise? A simple visit to a rectory reinforces their belief that the priest is not one of them. Even in the most modest parishes how many rectories make the workers feel that they are at home? The rectory may be very simple, the priest poor, but his room is either unfriendly and administrative, or has a bourgeois atmosphere even when modest. The priests who are aware of this fact live close to the people, preferably on the ground floor. Some are priest-workers; some, parish priests.

I cannot recall without emotion the tiny, drab living quarters in which I waited for an elderly priest who had pioneered for twenty-five years in eliminating the money problem. The room lacked the restful simplicity of a monk's cell. It might have been any very poor worker's room. The furnishings were reduced to the barest necessities—a small iron bed, a washstand, a desk, some shelves, two chairs. Towels were drying in the sun before the window, and some clothing hung on a nail behind the door. I knew of this man's titanic, lonely battle, his breadth of intellect and his depth of Christian charity. Surely, I thought, it must be simple for any working man to come here and talk to him while he sat at his battered desk. When Father "R" came, he did not sit behind the desk at all; he took a chair and brought it next to mine. Indeed, it must be even easier than I had thought for the workers to talk to him, man to man.

Later, as we were passing the Blessed Sacrament in the church, he prostrated himself, and I did the same. We prayed together for a few minutes. I was lost in reverence, crushed by a feeling of total unworthiness at kneeling with that man of God. It was as if I had touched saintliness.

I realized that the first requirement for a parish priest is to be poor among the poor—and in their fashion, not in the fashion of the poor bourgeois. "Go and sell all you have and give it to the poor." All you have: money, security, refinement, culture.

It may be objected that the churches are insecure, and have to depend on the collections and on contributions at marriages and funerals. "Ah!" says this priest, "That is just the point. We look like functionaries living off the sacraments. The whole atmosphere of the parish church is fouled by money. What dignity is left to the priest when he "has to discuss 'rates' for marriages, funerals and Masses for the repose of the souls of the dead?"

Many teams of parish priests started to do away with class distinctions—at their own risk, as the hierarchy had pointed out. Sometimes they did it of their own accord, without consulting the parishioners, while at other times the priests put it up to the parishioners for their decision. One priest, who was not a young man, had suffered in conscience for years over the whole problem of money. He himself was the son of a worker. At last, when his hair started to turn white, he decided he could stand it no longer. He went to his bishop and told him that he wanted to try and win back the workers' respect for the Church by placing the whole money question on a voluntary basis: no collection, no "price list." The bishop asked him if his curates were willing to try it. They were. The bishop replied, "It is at your own risk."

The priest's church ministered both to well-to-do-people and to factory workers, but was quiescent, having an active congregation of only a handful of faithful women. He summoned them and told them there were going to be several parish meetings. He showed them a map of all that part of town that his parish was supposed to cover. They remarked that there were few parishioners in that territory.

"I don't care if they don't attend church," he said, "I don't care if they haven't made their First Communion. I don't care if they are divorced. I don't care if they are improperly married. I don't care if they have been in prison. I want to talk to all who have been baptized."

He assigned a section of town to each woman and explained that they were to visit everybody who had been baptized. They were really to visit—not merely leave their card in the mailbox—and inform the people that there was going to be a meeting. In each section they were to find several homes which could accommodate from thirty to fifty people. In these homes the people were to meet.

The good women balked at first. It was an incredible situation, they said. He invoked his priestly authority and ordered them to do it. One of them obeyed and the rest followed.

The meetings were attended partly out of curiosity, partly because it was easier to go to a neighbor's house than to the church.

The priest made his message plain: "What is the parish church to you, an abstraction? Who owns it? You own it—not the building, but everything else. A parish is a big family. All of you, *all*, are my children, and I am father to all of you, rich and poor. Does it seem just to you that distinctions should be made among the children? More than that, we are all children of the same Father. Does it seem right to you that in His house there should be distinctions among His children? As far as I am concerned, I don't feel free to make distinctions any longer. You workers say that the priests try to sell something, and you are right. But that will not be so in the future. I am through. I will not do it again. I propose one class for all, rich and poor."

How did the rich people take it?" I asked.

"Surprisingly well. They said I made it much simpler for them, because, if they did not have first class ceremonies, the people said they were stingy, and, if they did, they said it was a shame to see such a display

101

of wealth. So they were criticized in any case. To have only one class would end it all."

"Of course, the poor liked it?"

"Yes, only we had some discussion about which class should be adopted. The poor wanted the first class! I said that it was for them to decide. Were we a family that could afford first class? When the carpet is worn out, can we replace it? Can we afford so many candles and things? It was up to them. They all talked it over, rich and poor alike, and finally the second class was adopted."

"Did they ask why you were willing to make such a change, when so many other priests were not?"

"Yes. But I said to them: Do you want to know why we priests have become merchants? When Church and State were separated, we lost our heads. Instead of truly relying on God, we preferred to arrange our little material life in our own way. And we did. Very well. So much for the carpet. So much for the hangings. So much for the organ. So much for a low Mass. So much for a high Mass. It is to our shame that we did not rely on God. From now on we are going to rely on Him in this parish. I do not mean to say that you should not give anything, but whatever you give will be entirely voluntary. It will be your offering to the family life. Of course, those who can't pay, don't pay. Each person offers what he can, through love of the community. If you are wealthy, you are only the steward of your riches. Use them; do not misuse them. Offer them in place of someone who can't offer anything. But everybody will have the same ceremonies."

"And if they did not give you anything after all?"

"I was asked that question, and I answered that I would be satisfied with less than would satisfy my poorest parishioners. Some of them knew this was true, because they had been to the rectory and had seen my room and seen me eat. There were no grounds for a myth of the rich priest in my community. If they would give me nothing, I said, my piece of bread would become so small I could not even share it. I would not judge them. Our Father in heaven would judge them."

So it was settled: no chairs, no collection (a box at the door), no classes; only voluntary contributions. There were real difficulties in the practical application of the principle: difficulties with the funeral parlors, the organist, the florist. With the help of his curates and the community everything was solved satisfactorily. The greatest problem arose in the case of a very wealthy marriage. They thought this idea of one class was all very fine, but *they* were willing to pay the organist and the florist.

"Then those beautiful ceremonies won't exist anymore?" said the bride. "I might just as well get married at six o'clock in the morning and wear a tailored suit."

"Yes, indeed," said the priest, "because what is important is the sacrament. You thought of your dress, the flowers, the music, but did you think of the sacrament?"

"But just the same, Father, weddings used to be so beautiful!"

"No. They were not Christian."

The priest persisted, and so did the community. Later on, he had to set up rules regarding flowers. At first, he could not exercise control over floral displays at weddings and funerals. Some could afford masses of flowers, some could not. So the rule was established that no more than four vases were allowed on the altar, the surplus to be put on the Blessed Virgin's altar, and all the flowers brought into the church belonged to the church. The priest was careful to schedule a poor marriage immediately after a rich marriage, so that the poor would have the benefit of the decorations."

"And how is the financial situation?" I asked him.

"It has never been better. But what pleases me most is the new atmosphere of the parish. Rich and poor have come to know each other. Everybody wants to do something. We have had meetings in various sections of the town to discuss other questions, and not only do the Christians come, but humanists and communists. People who had not set foot in the church for twenty-five or fifty years have come back. Many of them have a strange conception of the priest. They say: 'But, Father, we are divorced,' or 'I live an irregular life,' or 'I am an atheist.' And I tell them: 'You are still my children.' "

"What does the bishop think of your experiment?"

"He is so pleased that he has ordered the experiment to be tried in all five parishes of the town. But it is not an unusual experiment. I receive letters from colleagues all over France who are doing the same thing."

At another town I went to Mass in a church which had been named "St. James of the United States," because it stands amid endless groups of huge workers' apartment buildings, exactly the same in architecture, and similar to American structures. As I came in, I picked up a pamphlet for the service of the day and deposited my offering. Here, again, there was no collection. The young pastor thundered from the pulpit: "We are not directors of ceremonies, organizers of entertainments or concerts. We are here to help you pray and put Christ into your life."

Father "R" began his first experiment many years ago, when his quarter of the town was new, the church only a shack. He had overheard two workmen talking at the door and saying: "Watch. All these antics, it's only a way of getting money. Wait for the plate!" It would have been useless to explain to them that the collection was only a substitute for the general offering for bread and wine during the first centuries of the Church.

Father "R" wanted his church to be an expression of Christian communal life, but he realized that the money question barred the way. So he removed the bars. Every week a multigraphed account of the expenses and income of the parish church is distributed at the door. The congregation makes its offering in envelopes, anonymously dropped in the box at the entrance. The number of envelopes serves to give an idea of how many families contribute, but the pastor never knows who has contributed, nor how much. On the other hand, the parishioners know exactly what the money is used for.

Different parishes require different solutions to the financial question. In some places one collection is taken up quickly after the Credo by young men who bring all the offerings to the altar, as is done in certain Protestant churches in America, and there is none of that noisy emptying of coins which is so painfully disturbing.

Elsewhere, the abolition of classes has not quite come to maturity. Displays are left to funeral parlors or florists, but the religious ceremony proper is as elaborate for the poor as for the rich. Once the priests are willing to cast their lot with the poor people, things start to happen. It is perfectly true, of course, that collections are not for the priests, but for the church and its many works of mercy. But, to win back the confidence of the poor, one has to take some risk. Besides, there is real gain in reconsidering the works of mercy in the light of modern communal life. That is another question much beyond the scope of this book. The fact remains that, no matter how often it is explained to the workers that the collections and class rates are for the benefit of the destitute, some workers will continue to say of the priests—to quote Abbé Michonneau:

"It is their profession. It is clever, well planned, wisely organized, skillfully presented, so as to draw from credulous poor people a source of income. . . . Everything has a price. . . . It is a terrible condition, and it holds a fearful condemnation. How many good souls have been turned away by all these little scandals, which caused them to identify the Christian religion with the traffic of the merchants of the Temple whom Jesus drove away with a whip!"

And of the seating arrangements:

"The working man will not go and sit in the 'good seats.' Lucky for him! Seats are rented in the house of God. It is not a community of praying people, but a theater, where the people in the top balcony should not disturb those sitting in the orchestra. . . . And what is to be said of the custom of renting a seat for midnight Mass in some churches in Paris and in some of the provincial towns?"

"The workers see the Church as a moral power, well organized financially . . . not at all the power whose mission it is to spread Christ's word for the salvation of the world."

If the parish church continues to exact money from the workers, it will never bridge the gap between them and the priests. Regardless of the liturgical and biblical renewal, it will never become the center of expression of Christian communal life. The parish church will be on one side, the workers on the other. It will never be their church, their house, the house of God.

CHAPTER EIGHT

Liturgical and Biblical Renewal

LET US SUPPOSE FOR THE moment that the financial stumbling block is on the way toward being removed. We have, then, the proposition that Christians should meet together to pray and offer the Sacrifice. They will come of themselves, through conviction that Christian ideology has value for their *whole* lives. On the other hand, we have already mentioned what happens, or does not happen, when the people go to the parish church. To quote the words of the ecclesiastical convention of St. Flour:

"The Mass is boring. Deadly. We ask why people don't come. We should ask why they come at all: they can't see anything, they can't hear anything, they don't do anything."

Abbé Michonneau has more to say on the subject:

"The children are bored. . . . Just look at them and put yourself in their place. What is asked of them?

To be quiet. They know it, and they have a mediocre relish for such a mediocre requirement. The public listens. . . . Usually they do not understand. Not only do they not know the Latin (that's evident), but the Mass does not mean anything to them, even with a missal and a translation. To make it mean something to them they should participate with songs according to their own genius. The public is bored—bored with good will, but bored. . . . We are under the illusion that the faithful who are there profit by what we give them, whereas the truth is that they are politely bored and pray in an individualistic fashion when they pray at all.

"The mere presence of the people is a great help if it does not make them pray! . . . Do you think the present practice corresponds to the commandment of the Church? Canonically, yes, but can we be satisfied with a juridical religion? The parish is a unit. . . . It has prayers and a form of worship which are not individual but social in character. . . . Things should be organized so that the celebration be as communal and effective as possible."

What, then, can be done? Are we going to teach Gregorian music and the Latin tongue? To put life into the parish church is not a matter of devices, but of attitude. The parish should be a place for communal worship. There are many channels for communal expression, so many, in fact, that, for parishes that have become communal, these questions have lost their extreme importance.

It is well to remember at this point that the Mass has two parts. One part is for the Catechumens. The other part is for the faithful, the initiated, and an outsider, hearing this part without any previous knowledge, would not understand what is going on. What is worse yet is that people who have a primary knowledge of what is going on still cannot follow it.

Communal worship should not be so very difficult to bring about, even though the priest who is willing to try it does not have an easy time! He has to be on his toes every minute. But he does not have to drive the people to participate. "What is communal," says Abbé Michonneau, "answers to a deep instinct of the soul." There are dozens of methods which can be tried. They may be called extraliturgical, or paraliturgical.

At "L," on feastdays, the people bring their contributions at the offertory: the children bring their school work, in the form of notebooks, their leisure in the form of a balloon or skip-rope; the adults bring their tools, their pots and pans, their musical instruments. At Christmas time the *santons* (images of saints) are the adult people themselves: the postman, the bus driver, the railroad man, the factory worker, the garage attendant, all in their work uniforms, and the last baby to be baptized is wheeled down the aisle by his mother.

All of them, the whole community, participate actively in paying homage to Jesus.

At "H" the people enact a mystery play at Christmas time in front of the choir.

At "St. A." the play is the community's main preoccupation. Workers in overalls and housewives with their shopping bags put it on in front of the choir (the Blessed Sacrament is always kept in a special chapel at "St. A.").

The paraliturgical activities at "C" have been so successful that the parishioners have had them published, as an inspiration to other parishes. Christmas Eve, for example, is really Christmas Eve; there are speaking choirs, traditional tunes, symbolic figures. The celebration is joyful, yet thoughtful, and prepares admirably for midnight Mass. At the 1944 and 1945 celebrations, a curtain was stretched in front of the choir. The people sang songs. The first was "The World Needs a Savior." In front of the curtain walked people who represented war, the prisoners, the deported, the missing. Then the community sang "The Denial of the Savior," and people representing the denial at home, at work and in the heart appeared. The next song was "The Savior is Born" and the people who receive Him were portrayed: shepherds, workers, men of learning, businessmen. The scenes were enacted on an elevated platform, on which, at the end, workers of the community built the altar for midnight Mass.

Abbé Michonneau reports that Mother's Day also has become very popular in France. On this day the central aisle of the church at "C" is "reserved for mothers. In the middle, on a podium, is a cradle. . . . At the offertory the mothers come to offer at the altar pictures of their children. In the afternoon there is a solemn celebration and the Blessed Sacrament is brought to crown the cradle and bless all the mothers. After this very moving ceremony the children come and give their mothers the beautiful bouquet which they had waved along the procession of the Blessed Sacrament. . . ."

The same church holds a Gospel Festival. In the evening, when a number of unbelievers are present, a large choir, in company with the deacon, sings answers to the burning questions of the present day—and the words are taken directly from the Gospel.

There is also a Festival of the Mass, a Festival of the Missions, of Baptism (the occasion being collective baptisms), and of Work. The whole community takes active part in all. Fitting songs have been composed—not always good from the literary or musical point of view, but having the advantage of being up-to-date and direct and virile. They are difficult to translate, but they are all typical.

It is readily seen that, when people have joyfully

participated in those communal expressions of an extra-liturgical character, they are ready for the liturgical ones. Of course, it may mean that the usual dutiful parishioners are displeased, at least temporarily. But that cannot be helped. Either the parish church has to go communal and rediscover what it was in the beginning, although adapted to present needs, or else it will die gradually, politely, and with it a strong, natural cornerstone of the Christian community.

In speaking of the liturgy, and the Mass, especially, it is necessary to point out that it is hardly more familiar to the bourgeois than to the working class. It may be easier for them to follow in a missal, but their knowledge is usually insufficient to make active participation easy. The liturgical movement is not, of course, new. As Father Duployé states it: "In this liturgical movement we are only heirs. The history of the liturgical movements in France, Belgium and Germany shows that the movement is closely connected with the sure and uncompromising Catholic thought and work of Dom Guéranger, Abbot of Solesmes." The renewal reached the elite at the beginning of the century. But today the idea is to reach all the faithful.

It is with that in view that the Centre de Pastorale Liturgique was founded in 1943. Though composed of Dominicans, the Center works in collaboration with the Benedictines in France and with the great other European abbeys which have already done so much for the liturgical renewal: Maria-Laach, Mt. Cesar, Klosternenburg and others. Varied ways are devised so that the faithful be no longer "bored spectators," but "convinced actors."

There are priests who choose to go all over France "explaining" the Mass. Usually, the instruction period lasts a week in each town. Every evening, by eight-thirty, the church is full. The missionary priest trains the children of the town to help him. They are the ones who, one evening, will re-enact the first Mass, dressed in Jewish costumes, as of Easter, 33; on a second evening, the Roman people, as of Easter, 220; etc. "Our Mass Taken Apart": such is the title. During the week everything is explained historically: how it came to be, the meaning of the ornaments, the things used, the participation of the faithful. It is all done, not only with apostolic zeal, but with modern teaching methods and breathless artistic perfection. Some people are fearful that it will turn out to be a little ridiculous, this "Mass Taken Apart," with the children acting right in the Church as in a theater. But, though it is direct and simple, it does not depart from dignity, and the seriousness of the ten-year-old children puts many adults to shame. Once the liturgical week is over, the missionary priest leaves. But it has been sufficient. Faithful and priests want to go on. That is to say, they want a communal

Mass. Special publications help them to do so—not only special missals, but a monthly magazine whose title page is left blank so that each parish may have its own name printed on it. The magazine has beautiful photographs and catching titles: "The Mass is a *banquet*," "The Mass is a *sacrifice*," "The Mass is a *getting together*," "The Mass is a *festival*," "The Mass is a *conversation with God*," "The Mass is an *offering*," "The Mass is a *starting point*."

I wish I could quote the whole publication. It is filled to the brim with joy, strength, life. And this, after five years of horrors and starvation. Here are a few extracts:

"To go to Mass is to sit at the table around the host of the house with one's own brothers." (At "St. A." the communion rail is in a circle around the altar table. The priest faces the people, as in many French churches today.)

"Is the Mass sad? No. It is a lesson for us: Christianity is not a religion of death, but a religion of life. . . . Mass unites us with Christ's passion, but even more with His resurrection."

"The true Mass is the Mass sung. French people do not know how to sing. Learn to sing."

"Contrary to what many people think, Mass is a time for talking. And this is normal. Our Lord spoke when He celebrated the Last Supper, and His apostles

asked questions. A meal without talk would be sad. . . .
The priest reads, the faithful read or repeat the prayers.
. . . The faithful do not always understand, neither does
the priest, at least not at the beginning. And, even later,
neither priest nor faithful catch the full import of the
prayers. But gradually, through telling and retelling
them, the mind opens, the words become clearer, and
sometimes they appear in their whole brightness, which
is nothing less than the language of God."

"The first Christians did not go to Communion
with eyes downcast, lost in individual meditation. They
went singing toward the Lord's table, happy to feel one
another's elbows and not to be alone when receiving
Communion.

"Mass is the life of the world. . . . Most Christians
do not understand the gift made to them. . . .

As Abbé Michonneau puts it:

"Have they [who come to Mass] come simply to
acquit themselves of a duty and in order egoistically to
insure themselves of eternal salvation, or in order to
nourish themselves with a life they will have to give
away?"

I had seen communal Masses both in Paris and in
the provinces, always in churches that might have been
called "bourgeois." I said to a Dominican that I was
afraid active participation was impossible among less
educated people, and that, if that were the case, the

117

whole liturgical movement had no point. But I was unfamiliar at the time with the extraliturgical training and the missions. He thoroughly agreed with me that, unless it could bring living Christianity back to the working man, it was a failure. But he added: "It is already full of promise. You are enthusiastic over what you have seen in bourgeois churches. But why don't you try the 'red belt' in Paris? It is ten times more inspiring."

I called up the pastor of "C." What time is Mass on Sunday?"

"Eight o'clock."

It was some distance away. "Any other Masses?"

"Yes," said a scolding voice, "at nine and eleven. For sleepy people. You ought to come at eight."

I did. It was cold and pouring rain. The church stood in a muddy plot surrounded by very poor dwellings, many of them tumbling down. People entered briskly—workmen, children, housewives. In the light of the single candle (there are few candles left in France) I saw the altar facing the people, and, as decoration, a beautiful carpenter's plane on each side. Back of the altar, where there is usually a picture, was an imitation of stained glass in what looked like cellophane, depicting a map of the territorial unit of the parish! The people felt right at home, with their own quarters facing them there above the altar. On each chair was a battered copy of a missal, called *The Life of Christ within Us*, by Abbé Godin, who did so much for the workers while he lived. I shall quote a few lines from the foreword:

"To be a Christian is not to become a member of a 'party' which fights for the 'right ideas.' It is not to be 'respectable.' It is to give up one's own life to a cause, the cause of Christ; to a person, the Lord Jesus. To be a Christian is not to put on an overcoat for one hour on Sunday. One recognizes a Christian because of the practical and active way in which he loves his brothers. . . . When one does not follow instructions before using a delicate and complicated machine, one wrecks it, and the whole factory suffers. And it is the same for us, if we forget to love our brothers in a practical way. . . . Prayer is the carburetor of Christian life. This book will help you to pray and so will give you the means of being a Christian. But do not forget that it is in one's whole life that one is a Christian."

The booklet goes on in simple direct language which never tampers with the teaching of the Church. The book gives the whole Mass, with the responses in heavier type. Gay, light blue, intelligently presented, this book is entirely different from the usual abhorrent "church" manual. It is the same old teaching, but has such an up-to-date presentation that, when you have read it, whether you are mechanic or plumber or rag collector, you realize that Christianity is for you, as it was two thousand years ago. In that poor church of "C" the workers nearly shouted the responses; they sang gay popular tunes and came out heartily with the *Gloria,* the *Sanctus,* the *Credo,* the *Agnus Dei.* When we surged to the Communion table, it was, indeed, a Communion, not only of each one of us with Christ, but of each one with his fellows through Christ. It was a sacred meal taken together, a Last Supper enacted together. The partaking together was at least as important as the individual act. In the pulpit the pastor apostrophized his parishioners: "You don't know how to listen. *Look* at me! *Think!* Why don't you laugh when I say something funny?" He has now a public as responsive as the French theater-goers, yet it remains respectful. The intensity of the participation is grandiose. That poor church of "C" was full to the brim with imperishable wealth.

Everywhere in France where there were communal Masses the spirit was the thing. Methods varied. One congregation could answer in Latin. In another church the priest officiated at the altar in Latin, while another priest dialogued the Mass in French with the people. Elsewhere the people could recite part of the Mass in Latin, like the *Credo,* but had to dialogue the *Introibo* with another priest in French. Of course, nothing is done that is contrary to canonical rules. There are many changes which clergy and people would wish to make, but it is for the ecclesiastical authorities to decide. Still, a great deal is actually being done within the proper limits.

I can do little more than touch on the Gregorian chant. From what I have heard, the people are able to learn some of the standard verses. There is little polish in the performance, but it answers the requirements of communal Gregorian singing. Some ecclesiastical authorities in France are not adverse to the thought that liturgical musical expression might come from the people of today, something that will, at the same time, answer our present rhythm of living and yet have its root in the past. However much it might be desired, a new liturgical singing cannot be made up artificially, even by learned monks. Those who have the background necessary to create music fitted for the praise of God cannot do so unaided and closed in from the world. They have to be near the people and listen to them— and wait. Some Benedictines have chosen this hard path. They have left their monasteries and the beauty and culture which surrounded them. They have come down as teams to live with the people and work with them in parish churches. They want the "praise of God," with all that it implies in beauty and spirit, to be made to live among the people. This, they say, cannot be done individually. It takes one community to quicken another community. "So we live a communal life, praising God among the people. We try to make permissible adaptations, which take their ignorance into consideration and lose nothing of the initial beauty."

It is a tremendous work, truly, what is proverbially known in France as "Benedictine's work," implying endless patience and deep humility, coupled with profound esthetic knowledge, deep artistic sense and fervent spirituality. These Benedictines are well aware of the bourgeois rut into which the liturgy gradually slipped in France during the seventeenth, eighteenth and nineteenth centuries. They know that the formalism which Jesus fought returned and speeded up the divorce of Church and working class.

There is divided opinion with respect to Latin. The problem is not so pronounced in France as in the Anglo-Saxon countries, where the language of the people is further removed from Latin than is French. The usual argument that it is a comfort for travelers to find the Mass in Latin the world over has been discarded. In the first place it is not true; there are Roman Catholic churches where the vernacular is used. In the second place there is little sense of proportion in worrying about travelers who, even with our swift transportation, will always remain but a small part of a country's population.

A very interesting inquiry into the use of Latin

in the Breviary has been carried on by the magazine, *La Vie Spirituelle*. Secular and regular clergy, nuns and lay people have spoken their beliefs. Though it concerns the Breviary, it still is interesting for us, because it pertains to the Latin question in general. Some of the writers emphasize the fact that the "Church is Roman but not Latin" (Benedict XV); that the unity of the Church is not founded on Latin; that the intention of the Church is not to unite men from the outside— through language, rite and customs—but from the inside, in one faith in God, who saves us through Jesus Christ. Others argue that to use the vernacular will date the texts, and they will have to be rewritten after a few generations. (For instance, the French of the fifteenth century makes difficult reading today for the average man.) There are many other arguments on both sides, but they all agree that Latin should not be done away with completely, in any case, and that some parts of the Mass, such as *Introit,* Epistle and Gospel, could be read in the vernacular by a priest or a lay reader. It is agreed that all the people would gain by an adequate, modern and beautiful translation in juxtaposition to the Latin. But such a translation cannot be done without a charism, and at the present time the church suffers badly from poor translations. The problem is not nearly solved, but many people are working toward its solution.

What is true of the Mass is true of all the Sacraments: their inner necessity to all comes to be readily acknowledged. But the form of presentation is a stumbling block to many new French Catholics. The French temperament is not ruled by emotion and cleverness; it is ruled by intellect and feelings. Things have to be logically explained, and felt. In the last analysis, of course, that is why only Catholicism can satisfy it, since it is the one religion which never lets the intellect down and gives maximum play to the feelings. Were it otherwise, atheism or superstition would be the consequences.

Regarding the presentation of catechism the fact has to be faced that in France it is too often taught by people of good intention, but who lack real understanding of what they teach. The catechism is imposed upon the children without any reference to their lives, and the result is that they learn by rote. An effort is now under way to renew the methods of teaching and to evolve a Catechism text having a presentation based on actual teaching experience. At "C," for instance, the catechism is being rethought and rediscovered by priests and children together. The truths are the same, but they are in modern dress.

In France the State has left Thursday free for religious instruction. But the children are burdened with homework, and, if they also have to come to church to learn catechism, it becomes only another duty. So the curate takes his bicycle and collects groups of children. In summer they sit together in a backyard; in winter they crowd around a kitchen stove. And they talk. They talk about their lives, what they have done during the week, what they have been thinking. The children, of themselves, ask the great questions connected with man's destiny, and, of themselves, they discover the sacraments.

I was slightly surprised at this, but the young curate explained: "You have no idea. The children are breath-taking. The most transcendental dogmas come out of their lips, not, of course, in theological terms, but with all their import. That is, if the children feel free, if they consider you as an elder brother."

With respect to their own spiritual lives, the accent is placed on the sins of omission. It is what we have not done which has separated us from God, and, especially, what we have not done for others. The children readily grasp the truth that our most personal sins do not hurt ourselves alone, but other people, the whole community, even if our sins are secret; they lessen the spiritual power of the community. Sins of omissions can be much greater than sins of deliberate intentions. People are not, as a whole, deliberately cruel, for instance, but they do forget to be attentive to their neighbors' needs. The children are quick to realize what they have failed to do during the week. They usually don't mind thrashing it out with the priest and their companions. The latter always have suggestions and are, in fact, much more severe than the priest in their judgments. Children naturally tend to probe very deep in their self-examinations. One ten-year-old boy forcefully confessed that he had gone *two* days without thinking! He did not think at all during those two days! He did not know what had come over him!

The priest and the children make suggestions as to what penance should be done for their faults. Usually, it amounts to doing, during the week ahead, what was not done before, and praying. After the discussion the meeting is dismissed, but the children come back individually for formal confession and absolution. The priest asks if there was anything they had not said in front of their comrades, and usually there is not. He recalls the penance suggested, confirms it and gives absolution. Then he mounts his bicycle again and goes to another section of his parish. It is work, a great deal of work, but the reward is great. In the backyards, in the streets, children hail the curate and rush to him, shrieking to the others: "Come on, Father is here! Catechism!"

These are lucky children in the revitalized parishes, where solemn Communion takes the form of a "declaration of faith," a renewal of the promises of baptism. At "St. A" the boys and girls come to the altar three by three, dressed in long, white robes of coarse material. Each group of three makes the promise in unison. Then the priest turns and says: "You have heard so-and-so and his intentions. He is young; what are you going to do to help him keep his promise to live as a Christian?" The question is asked directly of the father, the mother, the godfather, the godmother, if they are there. And then the priest commends the children to the whole community. It is the community's responsibility to help them be Christians.

This simple, earnest ceremony is not too much to the liking of many parents, some of whom regard the solemn Communion as no more than an occasion for a good meal and, possibly, some drinking; or, perhaps, as a means of satisfying a well-to-do-grandmother, or as a chance to display a little family vanity. The curate stubbornly refuses to admit to solemn Communion any child unless he is ready for his profession of faith and unless his parents are willing to help him bear the responsibility. It does not matter if the child knows the catechism by heart.

"But Father," wail the parents, "what is Pierre's grandmother going to say? And we invited the whole family from the province! We had planned such a wonderful meal! And everybody else in our family has 'done' his solemn Communion. It makes Pierre look as if he was awfully bad!"

It takes a great deal of courage to withstand the tempest, but the curate is not wanting. He believes in a Christianity of life, not in dead gestures. He truly believes in the commandments of the Church. They are not a routine; they are the commandments of life, commandments of the One who said: I am the Way, the Truth and the Life.

In the new militant parish church, each of the sacraments receives the same thoughtful treatment. It is rethought in terms which "humanize it." The whole beautiful liturgy of baptism is explained beforehand— the significance of the gestures, the words, the solemnity of the promise made by the godparents. In several places it is done just before Mass, so that the whole community may be present.

It is the same for marriage. People are very surprised when the priest does not seem anxious to marry them. He has seldom, if ever, seen them at church. He asks quietly why they want to be married in the church. "Why, indeed," he says, "if you are not Christians?"

"But, Father, we have been baptized and have 'made' our first Communion, and we try to do our Easter duty!"

"Do you think that makes you Christians? What do you think it is to be a Christian?"

Well, they had never thought of it. . . . "But in our families, people always marry in the church."

"Yes. Still, you, yourself, admit that you never thought about what it is to be a Christian. Look, you'd better go and get married at the city hall. And later, if you really want to know more about being a Christian and want to be married in the church, you come back here."

Some are angry and never come back, but many do.

The man is non-committal; the young wife wants to come back.

"Well, Father, what is it to be a Christian?"

"First, it is to love; it is to have a fraternal feeling." They had expected anything but that answer, and they are won over. Their rediscovery of authentic Christianity has begun. They have embarked on a great adventure, and their lives will be broadened as never before. Their church wedding will be beautiful, not externally, but in spirit. Perhaps other couples will be with them at the altar, perhaps they will be alone, but the wedding will be celebrated before Mass, and the whole community will be there, actively participating. And the young couple will become part of the Christian community, the young communal home, where the door is always open, a plate is always set, and there is an ever-present willingness to give a hand to one's neighbor and a joyous eagerness to praise the Lord communally.

The funeral liturgy is also explained by the priests. The people are given translations of the psalms used, and they repeat them in French. The name of the deceased is mentioned aloud. Many so-called Christians, as well as atheists, have discovered Christianity at these funerals.

So, gradually, the liturgy is becoming the expression of communal worship in the parish church, and the sacraments are being rediscovered as a condition for a full Christian life.

The study of the Bible has been sadly neglected among Catholics in France since the Reformation. The Church did not encourage this study, not because the Bible at any point contradicted the teaching of the Church, but because the hierarchy felt apprehensive over the possibility of wanton misinterpretations which would inevitably result in a multiplication of sects. The pendulum swung so far that the ignorance of the average French Catholic regarding the Scriptures became quite shocking.

The biblical renewal moves on three fronts, intellectual, theological and parochial.

The first puts at the disposal of Catholic thinkers the findings of archaeology, philology, literary criticism and other sciences.

The theological effort brings the critical rediscovery of the Bible into beneficial juxtaposition to
theological thought. French Catholics are fully aware
of the splendid impetus given by Protestants of the
school of Bultmann, Dibelius, Cullmann and K. L.
Schmidt. Scientific criticism by the Protestants was
once a sheer destructive criticism. But even that helped,
because, having gone through that stage, some Protestants emerged cleansed and washed of fragmentarism
and ready to probe into a constructive criticism which
is of great help.

The parochial aspect of the biblical renewal centers
upon the function of the parish church in seeing to it
that the Old Testament is no longer an archaeological
curiosity, but living food for the soul.

The best introduction to the Old Testament has
been the Psalms. The people are already somewhat familiar with them. Each Sunday the Church designates
passages for meditation by the faithful. Vespers and
Complines are composed of Psalms, and many French
Catholics are acquainted with the Psalms of Penance
and the *De Profundis*. The Psalms lead to further reading in the Bible, perhaps to Isaiah and Ecclesiastes. Step
by step the people are introduced to the prophets and
the patriarchs. Perhaps much headway has not yet been
made, but it is important that the people gradually understand that Christianity did not come about full-

blown, that preparations for it were made by God over the centuries through a chosen people. The Old Testament is full of lessons and counterparts of the New Testament. Indeed, only through the Church can we understand the Bible, but, when we do understand it, all the richness of Israel is ours.

The Bible plays a part in festivals, most of which have their origin in Jewish festivals. Pamphlets and stories centering on the Bible are introduced, and study circles are arranged, varying in accordance with the people's degree of knowledge. The policy in these circles is to answer questions, not to shut them off. On the other hand, criticism is never made an end in itself. Delving into the "historical Jesus," as was done during the last century, is obsolete. It may have had its value at the time, but it is felt today that biblical study is valuable only insofar as it makes the living Christ more tangible. As a priest of a parish missionary community put it to me: "The people have come of age. When Christ comes back He will not be a child."

CHAPTER NINE

Apostolic Zeal

THE CITY OF "L" LAY AT MY feet—literally. Not a wall was more than knee-high. I stood in the center of what had been a lovely old town and surveyed the immense desolation. It was so much worse than I had imagined that I wept. People passed by briskly. Farther on, up the hill, I could make out the temporary shacks in which they lived. Three main buildings still stood, towering above the ruins— the cathedral, the carmel, and, on the hill, the basilica. They had emerged intact from the bombing and the fire which had swept the town. In their preservation some might see the hand of God sparing the "high mystic place" that "L" is.

Whatever the explanation, the carmel still stands and has been able to put some of its outer building at the disposal of the Mission of France. As I approached, the large double door was wide open, facing an im-

133

mense walled courtyard. The courtyard was crowded with men, some in clerical habits, some in civilian clothes. It was a noisy place, the men talking to one another, some running, some crossing the yard with laundry baskets, others with tools. There was laughing, whistling and a general carefree atmosphere. I asked one of them if I might see the Superior of the seminary. "Right away," he answered eagerly and dashed into the building. In the short time I waited, several men asked whether they could do anything for me. I expected the first young man to come back and tell me to follow him to the Superior's office, or to the parlor. But not at all. He came back with the Superior himself, who walked with swift, energetic steps that belied his white hair. Nobility, intelligence and kindness were on that face, and his manner was direct and unassuming.

The seminary of the Mission of France was founded in 1941 "to develop, not parochial pastors or curates, but missionaries." Missionaries for the whole of France. Originally, they were intended for the provinces, to counteract the isolation of the country priest, the dearth of vocations and the dechristianization of the country areas. But it was soon evident that city and country were one. There was a constant flow of people and ideas from one to the other, and the dechristianization in the cities was just as great as in the country, if not greater.

So today the Mission of France is for country and city alike.

The Superior explained how the seminary came to be:

"Civilization is suffering a gigantic cataclysm. We need not mourn it too much. Its inspiration was deeply materialistic. Pretending to lead man to a New Eden, it has led him to a bloody death, recognizing and cultivating in him only his carnal faculties of enjoyment. But what tumbles down has to be replaced. Will the Church be present at the reconstruction? Will she be able to win out with her conception of man and life? Will the result be Christian?

"The problem of educating the clergy to meet the claims of paganism—a dynamic clergy with a theology of conquest rather than an established church theology—and the problem of devising new methods of organizing a priestly community around the bishop (the principal solution and in accord with Christ's own plan), could be solved only after formative difficulties had been overcome. To create the new Mission of France, a seminary, first of all, was needed."

Men are trained by the Mission of France to become missionaries, not regular priests. They enter because they have a missionary vocation. They enter at all different stages of instruction and states of life. Some are eighteen and just out of school. Some come from other seminaries where they have gone as far as philosophy and theology, or even have completed their studies. Some have been ordained, some not. Some have served a parish, while some are starting from scratch, having felt their vocation in the midst of their laymen's work. All ages from eighteen to thirty-five are represented, all degrees of instruction, all geographical areas and all strata of society. At the time of my visit, the seminary was instructing, among others, a peasant, a railroad engineer, a converted Jew, a technician, a butcher. They, like all the seminarians, were there, as L. Augros has pointed out, not "to prepare for an examination, but to complete their specifically sacerdotal formation and to cultivate within themselves the apostolic and communal virtues. . . . The Mission of France cannot be carried out by free-lance priests. It is essentially a vast communal movement."

The future missionaries live in teams from the start. The teams are usually composed of five or six. Everything is held in common, including money. Every team has its problem, and not the least is scraping together enough funds for all the members of the team to stay at the seminary. Wealthy seminarians are a rarity. There are a good many priests who have managed to set aside a small amount from their meager parish stipend. When everything is pooled together for the team, it sometimes is apparent that one or more will have to quit after a year or so. The teams do manual work outside during vacation time and in that way make a little money.

I was walking with an earnest young priest through what had been the streets of the ruined town. We met groups of young men in civilian suits, pushing wheelbarrows, carrying wood, working with pick and shovel, and my companion would say, "Another of our teams." The key word at the seminary is "freedom"—freedom because they have "left" everything, freedom because of the boundless joy of the Gospel. Outside the regular schedule the future missionaries are free to do whatever they please. They come and go, put on habits or remain in civilian clothes. "They are not going to be monks," the Superior said. "They are going to be in the world. They have to learn how to live there." So they help the townspeople. They do all the manual work at the seminary, take care of the laundry and the floors and peel the vegetables. The Superior peels vegetables with the rest of them during the evening, and it is a grand opportunity for talking and joking.

"You see," said the young man, as we were coming down from the basilica, "we need Christians who astonish." And I remembered what I had once read: "Actually, Christianity is no longer dangerous. It holds only a conservative and defensive position. Nobody worries over the 'Catholic virus' as people might worry over the communist virus."

"We have to be shock troops," the young man went on. At that moment we turned a vicious steep corner on the slippery mud and were confronted with the spectacle of a horse trying desperately to pull a huge load of wood, while his master held the bridle and encouraged loudly. Before I knew it, the priest's breviary was lying in the mud by my feet, and he was rushing down the muddy hill. He came back with a big stone clutched against his habit, bent over and propped it up against the back wheel. Then, bracing himself against the wheel, he said to the man, "Now, go ahead, I'll give you a push." I stood there in the bitter winter afternoon, and I remembered an exactly similar story about St. Nicholas, except that St. Nicholas had used the bishop's staff for the purpose.

Such spontaneity is typical of the seminary. "Candidates," said the Superior, "should trust only in the Lord who calls them." Christ does not call His apostles into something that is already well organized. The work of God has always proceeded in the same way, through people who are ready to risk all to fulfill the task He has entrusted to them. They have always succeeded. What difficulties and disappointments there have been! But did not Christ give the example, on Calvary, of work which succeeds through failure?"

There are now three tiers of bunks in the seminary rooms, and so many applications have come in that the Superior is at a loss what to do, unless Providence intervenes.

The Mission of France is under the protection of St. Thérèse of Lisieux. It may seem strange that such a virile undertaking should have her for its patron saint. Unfortunately, a whole literature, coupled with nauseating art, has made many think of St. Thérèse as a pietistic, sweetish, disembodied little girl. On the contrary, she had a clear, strong, untrammeled conception of important problems, as saints often have, even without the technical knowledge normally required. One of her main concerns was the spiritual welfare of priests, and she consecrated her life to them as "their apostle." "For my mission," she said, "as for Joan of Arc's, the will of God will be done in spite of men's jealousy." Quoting these words of St. Thérèse, the Superior of the Seminary of the Mission of France concluded: "So we can be confident."

Throughout the pages of this book we have met several teams of the Mission of France. There are many more, both in town and country. The communal formula is still being widely discussed, but it does seem to work, and it lends itself to all variety of initiative and improvisation. One of the latest devices is the trailer. Of course, there is nothing sensational for an American in this. But in France it is revolutionary. Trailers have been associated only with gypsies and circus people.

When I told some friends that I had been trying to catch up with the priests' trailer, they looked at me dubiously. Its very novelty is one of the reasons why the trailer idea is a sensation. Wherever it stops, everybody wants to come and look. When I climbed the steps and opened the door I came upon the team eating. It was like a pullman. A table stood against the window, and a partition at the end of the little room allowed for a stove in the kitchenette. A young boy with the traditional white cap presided over the cooking. Later, I discovered that the boy-cook could turn out excellent pancakes, which I finally was persuaded to try, together with a cup of the inevitable *ersatz* coffee.

The trailer was a two-car affair. In one were the living room and kitchenette and, at the other end, with a separate entrance, the tiny chapel. The other car contained three tiny bedrooms and a washroom. In each bedroom were a desk, a chair and a washstand. The chair opened up as a bed, provided the desk was closed first. There were shelves and small cupboards in the wall. It reminded me of a ship, with not a fraction of space wasted. It was like a big toy, and the boys who designed it were immensely proud of it and are having the time of their life with it: all the more so because, when they had passed through one diocese, the bishop visited them and was so enthusiastic that he ordered six similar trailers to be built for his own work.

When, not seeing any engine, I asked one of the priests how they traveled from place to place, he replied: "Why should we have a motor? It would be too expensive. We do what the circus people do. When we want to travel, we ask the company which moves the fair and circus to send their tractor. But we spend several weeks in one place, in any case. We are the kind of missionaries that parish priests call upon once a year to come and wake the people up. Ordinarily, missionaries are a headache for poor pastors who can't make both ends meet. They feel nervous while the mission is going on, and the missionaries feel uncomfortable, too. But, apart from the finances, there is the question of visiting a parish we know nothing about, and "preaching" to people whom we do not know, and who very likely are the same faithful flock the year round. What good does it do to talk to them? Besides, we wanted to work as a team, and, if it was hard to meet the expense of one missionary priest, what would it be with a team? So we hit upon the idea of the trailer. No more bothering about living quarters. The trailer would be more accessible to the people than the rectory. Pastors and missionaries would both be independent. We could stay in one place a long time, get acquainted with the people, help start communal Christian groups."

I asked him how the parish priests liked it.

"They are delighted. It has relieved them of all the tedious material side of the mission. We do not ask for any money. We sell books and popular editions of the Gospel. Then we co-operate with the parish priests, helping them rethink their parish work. We go over their programs and plan visits, meetings, festivals. We give many festivals—out of doors when the weather permits. We divide the parish among the team members and go visiting from door to door. No money. Just friendly visits. We talk over everything, whatever is on people's minds. And we tell them that we are always "at home" in the evening. They can drop in when they want to. Men like the idea, and visitors crowd the trailer living room every night. If they come at dinner time, there is always a plate for them. That's why we hire a cook, because we always want to be able to offer them something.

"The idea is to help people come of age. They can. They have done it in much of their thinking. They are ready to come of age as Christians and take on their own responsibilities. The priest is delegated to be more of an intercessor than a chief."

Every age creates new orders fitted to its particular need and mentality. It is also true of today in France. Charles de Foucauld has inspired several new orders. This extraordinary man, who did not make one convert

142

during his whole life, has been responsible after his death for countless vocations.

One of the most interesting new orders is Les Petites Soeurs du Père de Foucauld. There is no proselytism; nothing but friendship. Their conception is very original: Father de Foucauld's concern, forging a link with the Moslems, is to be pursued through a "working fraternity." Here, as in so many other avenues of religious life in France, whether for clergy, new orders or lay people, the emphasis is put on "exemplary sanctification of common work." The Little Sisters work in factories, and at home for big concerns. The money is for their own support, but also for the support of the Little Sisters who are called to the Sahara desert.

I entered one of their houses, which was like any bourgeois house in France. A widow was living there, and she had given over the whole place, save her own room, to the Sisters. The Little Sister who received me was working at home, painting *santons* for a big firm. She invited me to dine with them and attend noon meditation when the Sisters who worked in the factories came home. She was very young, and she still wore the short dress of the postulant.

The door opened and the Little Sisters from the factory came in. Each wore a blue scarf on her head and had on a long blue working dress, reaching to about five inches from the floor. They could be taken for any working girls, were it not for the wooden cross hanging from their necks and the large, flamboyant red cross and Sacred Heart sewn on their breast. It was so unbelievably daring that it was magnificent. They were all young and gay.

We all went into the drawing room, which had been converted into an oratory. The altar stood at one end. The decorated armchairs and smaller, ornate chairs had been ranged against the wall, leaving a large carpeted space in the middle.

The Little Sisters knelt on the carpet and prostrated themselves after the manner of the Moslems. They prayed in Arabic, making the Sign of the Cross and reciting the Hail Mary in that language. Then they sang popular Arabic melodies. The Gospel was read, and there followed a fifteen-minute meditation. Some of the Sisters remained kneeling for this; others, without rising, relaxed on their heels, in oriental fashion. Their rules provide for much meditation, because it is a point of understanding with the Arabs, who also meditate much.

The atmosphere was most impressive and one clearly felt the double dedication of these young women to the working class and to the Moslems. They linked the French and Arab working classes, and were making possible the presence of Christianity in the middle of Islam.

They were, indeed, partaking fully in the lot of the working class. Their bare ankles were swollen, their hands cut with chilblains. We ate in the kitchen. It was the only place with a fire, except for a few sticks burning in the room where the Little Sister painted her *santons,* and, even at that, I suspected her of having lighted it for me. On the kitchen table were bowls and wooden spoons. Everything was designed to accustom them to the life they would lead if called to the Sahara mission. They learn to go without water, to use wooden spoons and to eat everything from one dish.

"What factories do you work in?" I asked.

"In an electric bulb factory and a cleaning and dyeing establishment."

"Did your cross and Sacred Heart cause you trouble?"

"A little, on the first day. Some workers laughed. Others did not want to have anything to do with us. But after that it was easy. The novelty wore off, and they accepted us."

"What is your schedule?"

"We work from seven to twelve and from two to six. We rise at five for meditation and Mass. We go to bed at nine-thirty."

"Are you on friendly terms with the other workers, or do they leave you by yourself?"

"Oh, no. We are just like one of them, especially,

of course, those of us who come from the working class. It is a little harder for the others. But all the women are friendly and respectful. Some of them call us "Sister," but others use our first names. It doesn't matter. We are just like them, depending entirely on our day's work for a livelihood for ourselves and the Sahara community. Dowries are not accepted in our order, so we are just as insecure as the working class. They realize this and have accepted us. Everyone knows about our 'working fraternity.' "

"Which of you will go to the Sahara?"

"We don't know. It is for the Mother Superior to decide. But those who are designated have to go and study three years in our Tunis house to familiarize themselves with Arabic and the Islamic civilization."

"So, you have specialized in the Islamic mission?"

"Not at all! Les Petites Soeurs du Père de Foucauld go *anywhere*. We are ready for the most unheard-of places and any sort of daring adventure. That is a requisite for membership. Who knows? Perhaps we shall be called tomorrow to the North Pole, or to India, perhaps even to America!"

The Petits Frères du Père de Foucauld (Little Brothers of Father de Foucauld) operate on the same plan as the Little Sisters. In the desert they are to be only a few miles from the Little Sisters, so that they can render each other assistance. No distinction is made between the Little Brothers who are priests and those who are not.

Again I went to a house like any other. It was hard to find in the factory suburb, where the streets were so badly lighted. But the minute I was inside I forgot the cold night. I was surrounded by extraordinary faces. Some of the women were very young, some middle-aged. They were dressed like anybody else, in no way distinctive excepting for the peace and joy of their expressions. They were the Carmélites dans le Monde (Carmelites in the World). Their aim was to live a contemplative life in the world: no proselytism, no outside apostolate. They wanted just to be. The Carmelites are in the world, but detached from their immediate surroundings. To them contemplative life may help someone in Timbuktu or Shanghai, in accordance with God's will. So far, their teams have settled in communist surroundings or in particularly corrupt places like tourist centers. But tomorrow they might be sent to a small bourgeois town.

As they are all working girls, they have to settle in places where there are varied opportunities for earning a livelihood. All the girls work outside: in business, or as teachers, secretaries, nurses, cleaning women or factory workers. There is no age limit and, of course, no class distinction. After three years as novices they all must give their worldly possessions to other people and join the team with absolutely nothing except a capacity for work. The Carmelites are afraid of giving in to what they have seen in other orders, namely, a hardening, a settling down to routine. So they have no set rules and no formal vows. After three years, if it is decided that the novice may join, she solemnly renews, before the whole community, her baptismal vows.

They have no fixed communal prayer hour, except on Sunday, but they hear daily Mass at the parish church. Periodically, the community meets to discuss the spiritual state of the members. Any fault is first considered on the premise that the community has failed to understand or help the member transgressor. The standard of living is based on that of the lowest wage earner in the neighborhood. Funds over and above the minimum requirement are given away. Although they dress like others, their clothes do not belong to them. Clothing is fitted and distributed at the beginning of each season, but before another year comes around it has very likely been allotted to another member of the team or given away outside. The same holds true of their jobs. The team might reach the unanimous decision that a member must quit her business assignment and take up a cleaning woman's job. Of course, the same things occur in ordinary convents, but it is not so easy to practice such detachment when one works in the world. Rule or no rule, it is a very difficult way to perfection.

I sat with the Carmelites and a Dominican priest at a large table. The meal was simple and good and the talk intelligent and gay. I looked about at them. Here they were, poised above an abyss. They had no material certainties. They were not even sure that their order would survive. They had nothing but their dedication to a cause, and team support—and grace. It was, indeed, a dare-devil enterprise. Was it the fullness of their relinquishment which gave them such freedom, and a certain positive quality of purity which gave them a stronger consciousness of reality?

All of them were charming. There was every sort of hair-do: the plain knot at the back, shingle bobs and permanents. We all had a good laugh when a young member, secretary to a communist municipal council, told us that one of her employers said she was good enough to belong to the Party. The council knows that she is a Carmelite. They deplore it or admire it, but are highly pleased with her professional services. The Carmelites in the World are very hospitable and they have a great variety of dinner guests. They are frightened of nobody, regardless of profession or ideology. Even so, they might have had a harder time balancing on their tightrope if the Dominicans and the hierarchy had not been moved to give them friendly and powerful spiritual support.

The Dominicans in the World have much in common with the Carmelites in the World. They dress in everyday clothes, and their confessor advises them to choose gay colors, in line with Frenchwomen's natural reaction against the sadness of the war years. The Dominicans in the World attend to all the social services of a large town: health, children, unemployed, factory workers' problems. It is their profession to do so. They live on a regular salary. At home, wearing a long uniform apron and a scarf on their heads, they file into their chapel to say the Office.

Just as there are non-cloistered Benedictine monks, there are non-cloistered Benedictine ladies. Full-fledged Benedictines as to habit and vows, they have opened their convent to the outside so that the rule of St. Benedict might penetrate the world. They receive temporary guests, groups of working girls, brides-to-be, married women who need time for recollection. The guests eat with the community. They attend services and, if they desire, they are initiated privately in the Office. The convent houses the Secretariat of Le Centre de Pastorale Liturgique, which is largely responsible for the liturgical renewal.

The vigorous work of French laymen must also be considered. Catholic charities are not properly included in this missionary movement, nor is social work. The Church is not a club. But there is a strong tendency today to develop Catholic charities and social work as a communal endeavor, Christian families being directly responsible for so many people.

Many lay people are engaged in some specialized movement of Catholic Action, such as the JOC, JAC, and JEC (Young Catholic Students). These movements are abandoning proselytism and seeking primarily to raise the material and spiritual level of living. It is being done in many different ways. I have not even mentioned, for example, the JICF (Young Independent Catholic Women), which compasses the small bourgeois, the upper bourgeois and the old aristocracy. Recently, the JICF launched a campaign to pool precious family jewels to make chalices, "to atone for sins of luxury."

A great deal has been accomplished through the lively intellectual effort of the JEC, who have published book after book on the professions, which they have rethought in terms of the Gospel, the technical side fully up-to-date and a fearless Christianity of life set in bold relief.

A courageous and informed sense of justice permeates all Catholic action, which, of course, has what the nonchristian movements have not, namely, charity. Many lay people are not formally organized because organization means routine and immobility, but they are counted on in the missionary movement and actively participate in it according to their ability and calling.

Some lay people devote themselves to discussing religion with their neighbors. People do want to discuss religion. The "train's destination" is on everyone's mind, even if it is to deny that there is any destination. And when one's parents have suffered from nineteenth-century clericalism, coupled with clever propaganda, one hardly cares to talk with a priest, but one is not adverse to talking with a lay person.

Another plan is now under contemplation whereby women will be trained in modern methods of pedagogy and religious criticism in order to become paid catechists.

The whole lay apostolate is centered about the bishop. More and more laymen have access to the bishopric. The bishop calls them in singly or in groups to discuss current problems. He also receives the vows of men and women who want to offer their lay life to God, who want to consecrate themselves wholly, but whose particular circumstances do not allow them to join any team. They are dispersed throughout France and keep in touch with each other through bulletins, letters and retreats. The bishopric is becoming the center and inspiration of the lay people. And there are many bishops, some of them advanced in years, who are not afraid of being "Christians who astonish."

The Boimondau Community

VERY FEW PEOPLE HAVE HAD
the privilege, in the modern world, of seeing genuinely
free men. I have seen them in a French factory. It is
an unforgettable experience to observe an entire group
of human beings carrying themselves with dignity, as-
surance and freedom. It was a unique atmosphere,
brimful of hard work, initiative and joy.

The founder of the Boimondau Community is a
working man himself. His idea has not been to create a
new form of plant nor to unite the workers in a profit-
sharing plan and do away with salaries. "Any solution
which will simply aim at a repartition of wealth," he has
said, "will fail sooner or later. What one should be after
is a society for men. We are not a plant. We include a plant." What he sought was a solution which
would give man the maximum of human life and
do away with the separate little units in which he is now

forced to live. In simple, direct language he tells how his idea developed:

"Family: complete misery. I left home. It was during the war of 1914. I lived under dreadful conditions, sometimes walking the streets without shoes. . . . I was in an orphanage for a while; then I entered the seminary. I thought I had a vocation. I found that I was mistaken, and I did the only honest thing and said I was mistaken. They did not keep me. I experienced the sorrow of not being able to continue with my studies for lack of money. I learned a manual trade and went to work. It was a struggle to win the respect of the other men. I saw at first hand what bosses could be like, and what the workers were like. My wife and I soon decided to go on our own. At least we could provide an example to people of what could be done independently."

So they sold their furniture and bought machinery for the manufacture of watch casings. For six years he and his wife were not to enjoy more than three or four hours of sleep a night. They had no money in reserve, and the banks refused to give them a loan. "I don't know," he said once, "if you can realize how outraged a man can feel when he knows that he has capacity for his work, and everything is corked up because there is no money."

Even under this terrible stress he tried to arouse in his workers a desire for a more human, balanced life.

154

He was an authentic Catholic—not merely a church-goer, but an ardent, dynamic Christian. The young workers were impressed with his efforts on their behalf, but their parents continually threw cold water on their enthusiasm, and they gave up.

He moved to another locality where there were several youth organizations, and there he hoped to find some response. But the young men were still frightened; they were not ready for such an adventure.

After the armistice in 1940 he moved on again, and set up his machinery in a barn. He could not find any workers skilled in the manufacture of watch casings, so he set about training men for the work. He rounded up a plasterer, a sausage maker, a waiter—all unskilled labor—and told them that, if they wanted to work with him, they would have to devise some means of eliminating the employer-worker relationship. He would not take them on until they promised to apply themselves to finding a more complete, harmonious way of life. They agreed, and things soon started to happen.

"First," he said, "there was the problem of finding a way of life which would enable us to respect each other and above all to make us grow. It was decided that the best beginning would be to allow each one to tell the other off. We met frequently and sought to build by unanimous decision rules for the community. In time, we felt, these rules would not be looked upon as outward compulsion, since we would all have accepted them. We quickly saw the need of a common ethic. We were all different. We saw that our ethics were not identical, but we sought to discover what they had in common and we reached the decision that the laws of the community should have as a basis that minimum ethic to which we could all agree. Those who had stricter standards, like the Christians, were expected to live by them, but they did not have the right to impose them on anyone else."

The difficulty of arousing workers to a truly better way of life is general, and France is no exception. They prefer to leave things as they are and to rely on others to make the wheels go round. Many of them are content to slave along in their golden shackles. They are satisfied with the high salaries which go hand in hand with serfdom or, at best, with passive obedience to the party and the labor unions. They want someone to take charge. They don't have the will to work out their own freedom.

There are, of course, some workers who prefer a system which allows them to exercise their own initiative and develop themselves to the maximum of their potentialities. Communism does not offer them any such freedom. It does claim that annihilation of the human personality is a temporary phase, but the more intelligent workers wonder how temporary the phase will be. They do know, however vaguely, that authentic Christianity restores men's natural freedom. Even so, the first strivings of a Christian order will find support from few workers, and fewer employers.

At Boimondau, where progress was at last being made, the workers began to feel the need of a better education. They satisfied the need in stages. First came physical culture, then music, French grammar and bookkeeping. Other subjects were added in the order in which the need arose. The first question to be faced was: When would the workers be able to study? A certain level of production had to be maintained, the workers had to put in a certain number of hours to maintain that level, and they had little time or energy left for study when the day was done. The solution was to gain time on production and to use for educational pursuits the time saved by speed-ups and short cuts. The men were so eager that the production tripled. Teachers were brought to the factory and classes held on the premises. At the time of my visit the men were working on a forty-five-hour-week basis. But they managed to save six of these hours a week, and this time was devoted to education. They were paid by the community for their hours of study at the same rate as they were paid for working.

Boimondau is not merely a factory, or even an economic set-up for the fight against capitalism. It is essentially a new organism in a new society. "It is a community of men, the human cell of a human society," as the founder insists.

It is not a co-operative. In a co-operative what binds the members together is only material advantage. It is not a communistic experience. Boimondau is founded neither on partisan ideology nor on class struggle. There are no stockholders, and the workers are not the owners of fractions of the community. On the other hand, it is not a development of the *phalanstery* idea, a peaceful, humanitarian, evangelical grouping apart from the world. To the contrary, it inserts itself vigorously into the concerns of everyday modern life.

After the young workers of Boimondau had thought out, discussed and finally lived their plan, and found that they were undergoing steady, complete development, they agreed that the means of production should be held in common. The owner, who had organized the community with such heroic determination in the face of terrible hardship, contributed the whole factory to the community, to be operated even more for the common benefit than was done before.

Recalling that M. B., the founder, had eight children, I said to the member of the community who was telling me the story:

"M. B. disinherited his children, didn't he?"

"You mean, from a capitalist point of view?"

"Yes."

"He did. But he is a Christian!"

That summed up the situation, and rightly, because it is said that M. B. knows three things very well: his manual trade, the Gospel and the teachings of the Church. How, then, can he do away with the capitalist system, when the Church has always defended the right to private property? Neither M. B. nor the Boimondau Community is against private property. What they want is that all workers should have access to the private property of goods for use and consumption, provided that the property is the legitimate fruit of their work. The Church, they point out, has always defended private property as one of the indestructible rights of men, but she has never said that the form adopted had to be the capitalist system.

M. B.'s gesture is considered by the community as a symbol, as well as an example: "We do not intend to despoil the capitalists. We shall gradually give them back their capital through the fruits of our work."

A representative of this new communal movement has put before the Constituent Assembly a proposed law which would transform the country from a capitalist to a communal regime. Needless to say, the proposal was no more popular among the communists than with the capitalists. At Boimondau, where there are eleven communists among the 167 workers, one of the Party members said to me, with enthusiasm: "No, the Party is none too pleased with us here. It accuses us of running off with their revolution. We have skipped the overthrow of capitalism, the class struggle and the dictatorship of the proletariat, and in one leap we have arrived at 'communism.' We just laugh at them and say, 'Too bad, old man, you communists are way behind us!'"

It is interesting to analyze the components of the Boimondau Community at the present time. There are one hundred families, comprising 280 people. Seventy of these people are avowed materialists, fifty-eight humanists, forty-two Protestants and 110 Catholics. These figures are known with such accuracy because anyone desiring to enter the community is first required to state his position with respect to man's place and destiny. It is inconceivable, say the Boimondau workers, that people should not think about this, for the same reason that the passengers on a train must have ideas as to their destinations. Provision is made for all members to study their philosophies of life or to clarify and develop their religious convictions. One hour out of the six devoted to study each week is given over to the study of Marxism for the Marxists, general philosophy for the humanists or religion for the Christians.

For the Catholic group, a Mass is conveniently celebrated every Sunday in one of Boimondau's factory rooms. A working bench is covered with the altar cloth and a cross has been made with watch casings. The workers stand about the altar table. They answer the priest-worker and with him they discuss the Epistle and the Gospel. Afterwards the fellows put everything in order, set a table cloth over the working bench, and they all have breakfast together there with the priest. The young Catholic worker who was telling me about this was radiant, and the others, humanists and materialists alike, shook their heads gently and said "Yes, the Catholic fellows, they have something there."

The minimum body of ethics by which the community lives is subscribed to by every member and enforced by a pledge. The workers promise to reform their private, public and family lives according to the accepted code of ethics. They likewise help others to carry through their reforms. Finally, they pledge themselves to complete tolerance and respect toward different ways of belief, holding that each one has the right fully to follow the practices of his own religion. The community further pledges itself to facilitate study and to help others in the search for a more complete faith or philosophy.

At this point I should like to quote a few extracts from the Boimondau rule of common ethics:

(1) Man cannot live without an ideal. Every per-

son will adopt an aim for his life, and will be prepared at any time to explain his choice.

(2) Man has spiritual, intellectual and physical faculties. He should cultivate them all. He is free to choose his own method of doing so but he should do it.

(3) Each member is bound to respect the following ethical rules adopted by the community:

Thou shalt love thy neighbor.

Thou shalt not kill.

Thou shalt not rob thy neighbor.

Thou shalt not lie.

Thou shalt be faithful to thy promises.

Thou shalt earn thy bread by the sweat of thy brow.

Thou shalt respect thy neighbor, his person and his liberty.

Thou shalt respect thy own self.

Thou shalt fight in thyself the vices which degrade man, the passions which hold man in slavery and hinder social life, and the vices of conceit, greed, lewdness, envy, gluttony, anger and laziness.

Thou shalt hold that there are goods superior to life itself: liberty, human dignity, truth and justice.

It becomes clear that the community is not composed of a select group, but of individuals who will accept its basic premises and work with energy and good will toward the ideal. "The man who is selected as

162

chief of the community," says the platform, "is the best man, having the highest totality of human value. He gives example, educates, loves, devotes himself, serves. To obey a chief who is wanting in these qualities is cowardice. What is required of the chief is also required, comparatively, from all members of the community. Men are equal in nature, but not in value. They have not all received the same gifts, nor in the same degree. They must be willing to be classified by the community according to their total human value."

The system of remuneration stems from these premises. Men are compensated not only for their professional ability, but also for their social, cultural and physical value, their value as comrades and what is called their "counter-effort" value. The last-named term designates the quality of the work that they are obliged to perform for ten days every three months at the community farm. The conception of "work," then, has been broadly extended to include the whole man. It takes into consideration his family as well as himself. His wife appears on the payroll and is paid on the basis of her total human value and family status. A young married woman without a child, for example, is gauged differently from a married woman with children. Homemaking is work, and is recognized as such. Wives have the right and the opportunity to become members of the community.

Even the children, from the moment that their conception has been medically certified, are recognized as members of the community and are paid. Their work is to grow. The sick are paid. Their work is to get well. Old people will be paid. Their work will be to retell their experiences and give advice.

The community members do not live together. They are integrated with the world. They may live anywhere within convenient distance of their work. Those who live in a certain section meet once a week at one another's homes and discuss community matters. This brings together all those who normally do not see one another in the course of the day. Wives, for example, who spend their days at home, meet the men and women of the factory. The meetings are directed by the chief of the section, who has been elected unanimously by the members on proposal from the higher authorities, thus avoiding demagogy and authoritarianism.

Community conflicts are referred to the community court, which is elected for one year and passes judgment on the basis of the common ethic and common sense. The court does not judge the fault, but the man, so that the same fault might receive different penalties.

A general council, which is made up of members of the court, the chiefs of the commercial services and the industrial, social and agricultural services, controls the community chief and enforces decisions. There is also a general assembly, which comprises all members of the community, although children, apprentices and postulants (applicants who are not yet full-fledged members) cannot vote. All unanimous decisions become law for the community. There are also weekly contact assemblies, where all general questions pertaining to the community are discussed.

The community chief is elected for a three-year term and exercises absolute executive power. But his powers can be taken away by the general assembly.

Many criticisms have been leveled at Boimondau and the system in general. Boimondau is at once a strong and very delicate organism, inasmuch as it takes into consideration the whole man. Christian in its conception, Boimondau might well degenerate into a tyranny if its chief were not himself an authentic Christian. But then it would have ceased to be Boimondau. It is not within the scope of this book to inquire into all the objections which could be raised against the system, but it is well to caution its opponents not to criticize it unless they are, in the first place, open to constructive proposals for the betterment of man. Criticism must not be based, explicitly or implicitly, on the assumption that no scheme can be accepted which differs radically from the systems in effect today. Boimondau does not advocate the bloody overthrow of capitalism. It does advocate a revolution in the spirit of capitalist and worker, and has put it into practice. Once the willingness to effect such a revolution of the spirit has been generally accepted, the forms of expression will come about gradually. They need not duplicate Boimondau. But they must aim basically at terminating the long-standing divorce between the concern for material progress and the concern for man. It looks as if they were to be the dissolvent of fascism, communism and capitalism. And they must, like Boimondau from which they derive, boldly encompass all the potentialities of man as a child of God.

The Boimondau idea is already spreading. There has been a national convention in Paris of the Rassemblement Communautaire Français, and communities are sprouting up in city and rural areas. The initiative is with the workers in some cases, with the capitalists in others. The communities are organized on the same basic assumption upon which Boimondau was built, namely, that the nature and destiny of man, rather than the economic structure, are the first consideration. Large plants will handle the change through the medium of small autonomous sections, so that proper living conditions can be restored without endangering mass production. No large plants had yet been taken over entirely, at the time of my visit, but communities within the plants were well under way, and the workers were consolidating their gains before acting to take over from the owners.

Some of the capitalists are alarmed at the prospect of losing their businesses to the workers. One owner to whom I spoke, however, a contractor in his late thirties, was distinctly friendly to the idea.

"Capitalists are crazy," he said. "They think that, if they go communal, they will lose everything, right down to their car and their bathtub. Actually, if they really knew their business, they could easily be elected communal chief at a high salary. The workers want chiefs who have experience and ability."

This owner had given over his plant to the community, and I asked him what his reasons were for doing so. "I heard a talk given by the founder of Boimondau," he replied, "and I was so enthusiastic that I talked about it all night to my wife. My business was doing very well, but the workers were not really happy. It made no difference when I raised salaries all around. I could feel their attitude. They arrived late to work, did as little as possible, collected their tools fifteen minutes before closing time. As a matter of fact, I had been thinking over the whole problem for years. The men were not living real human lives, and when the founder of Boimondau declared to the Catholic corporation heads that they were guilty of grave sin if they did not go communal, I could see the seriousness of the whole thing. I am not a Christian myself. I suppose I'm a humanist. But I could see eye to eye with him on what he said."

"Did you give up everything when the community took over your business?" I asked.

"No, I didn't. I told you I am not a Christian. But what interested me was the fact that the idea could be adapted to different circumstances. I could see that something could be worked out in my business. But I had not foreseen how hard it would be to convince the workers to take hold of the idea. It was not easy to wake them out of their torpor and make them want to be free through their own efforts, rather than look for freedom through State or Party legislation. I had to convince them that they had to work it out for themselves, that no State or Party could do it for them, even if it wanted to."

"Didn't they suspect your motives?"

"Yes, some did. It took me months to win their confidence. It was a long time before we could all lay our cards on the table. When they insisted that there must be some profit motive lurking back of my proposals, I said that they were perfectly right. They wanted to do good turns for others now and then, and I did, too. I wanted to do them a good turn, and at the same time I could profit from it. Taxes would be less, for one thing. Then, since everyone was looking for a broader, more fraternal way of life, why shouldn't we all try to do it together voluntarily, instead of waiting for some violent governmental house-cleaning, which would curtail our freedom and subject us to tyranny? Finally, they were won over, and we prepared the way for the community to take over the contracting business. We discussed and appropriated the ethical concepts of the Boimondau group, and adopted their system of remuneration and most of their principles and practices of life. The educational aspects, particularly, appealed to the men. Some of them could not read; others wanted to learn mathematics, and mechanical drawing, and various technical subjects. As at Boimondau, the educational program was incorporated in the working hours and the men were paid at the same rate."

"How is it working out?"

"Don't ask me that! The changeover is too recent. We have agreed to try it. The men have voted me in as chief, and, if the whole idea works out, they will gradually reimburse me for the tools and equipment. But this much I can say: It is now a pleasure to work with the men. They don't come late any more, they're as happy as larks, anxious to work and looking for improvements in their way of life. They have regular meetings in the various sections of town where they live, and the women, who were shy at first, come up with suggestions. It is all very dynamic, as life should be. I am having the time of my life! If every capitalist could realize what fun it is, he would go for it right off. This is the time to do it."

"Supposing," I asked him, "that at some time in the future a new chief were elected in your place. Then what?"

"That doesn't worry me too much. In the first place, it won't happen at all until someone comes along who has the experience needed for the job, and that's a long way off. But, if it should come about, I shouldn't want to work with men who did not want me as their chief. Besides, I should not be so badly off. All my life I have had so much more than any of these men. Probably I should start all over again in some other place."

"You do run a risk, then."

"Surely. It's worth it, though. Don't you Christians believe that the authentic Christian life is a dangerous one?"

Later, I came across a printer who was trying the communal scheme. He was taking on unskilled laborers, prisoners and deportees, and teaching them the trade. The community gave them the communal, individual kind of life they were longing for. Their rules are basically the same as at Boimondau, but they still are too poor to include wives and children on the payroll. But at the end of the year they will divide among the women and children whatever money is left.

There are communities which have been established without, as yet, any definite economic expression. But they are very active in developing certain economic efforts along various lines. They acquire a piece of property to start a communal factory when the time is ripe. They raise funds to set up a community of artisans. They distribute food. There is even a communal police force.

Discussion of the Boimondau idea is rife in many places. Workers and employers meet at dinners to discuss the possibility of activating a community. Usually the meetings follow a set plan. Three business heads meet with three Christian workers, three communists and, if possible, a union representative and a priest-worker—sometimes, too, a Protestant minister. Employers who are unwilling to part with their equipment have offered money to start communities in which they will not personally participate in any capacity.

Meanwhile, the founder of Boimondau travels about France, stirring up interest in his idea. Inspired and practical at the same time, utterly devoid of personal ambition, burning with zeal, he delivers his message in harsh, prophetic words. It was reported that at one gathering of large industrial concerns the men turned green with fright and the women fainted. And the communists wagged their heads and said: "See, they won't listen! They won't go the Christian way! We shall have to take over!"

But he goes on with his project, stopping at town after town. He is getting results, even though he is making enemies. He has suffered and he has made his stand against opposition. In 1944 the Germans set fire to Boimondau. Two of the community died in deportation, one was shot; of those imprisoned, three were rescued and two escaped. The founder himself was at Buchenwald.

Boimondau survives, happy and prosperous. Nevertheless, successful as it is now, it is wise to consider it still as an experiment, but as an experiment of great value—the kind that cannot be shelved, labelled and forgotten. In France, because of it, many industrialists and working men, Christians and communists, are uneasy. "Boimondau is the firecracker in the house," as a Carmelite has expressed it. Something is happening. And it works. Were it not to work tomorrow, it yet would remain a challenge to all and a definite step toward a human way of living fitted to our age. Boimondau gives a certain spirit, a direction, stemming from Christianity.

CHAPTER ELEVEN

The Protestant Renewal

THE NUMBER OF FRENCH PROT-
estants can be set between 600,000 and 800,000 at the
present time. This is a small minority, but more homo-
geneous than American Protestantism. There are a few
dissident churches, but the majority of members are
Calvinists and Lutherans, the former being called the
Reformed Church. Three centuries of persecution have
contributed greatly to the courage, indomitable will
and steadfastness of the French Protestants. Their rejection of the Catholic Church, based sincerely but er-
roneously on the notion that Catholic practice "took
something away from God," has led them to an in-
transigent concept of truth and a worship of literal
truth.

The consequences of their literal concept of what
does or does not "take something away from God" have
been various and devastating. We can only mention

here those which bear particularly on this present renewal. Statues, candles, stained glass, flowers, kneeling benches and even the cross have at one time or another been discarded as "untrue." Protestant services retained a communion service, but only at rare intervals during the year. Except for the commendable practice of choral singing, and the collective confession of sins, the Protestant churches encouraged, at least on Sunday, no active participation in the services on the part of the congregation. Monasteries, religious orders, rules for the spiritual life were, of course, done away with. The result was a religion of extreme individualism and a worship utterly devoid of externals. Liturgy was reduced to a skeleton.

Long before the present renewal French Protestants heard within their midst the voices of great spiritual leaders. Vinet and W. Monod advocated a better understanding of what had been common Christian experience prior to the sixteenth century, not as a return to the past, but as an acceptance of Christian acquisitions. The influence of Karl Barth was twofold. For some it meant a definite swing away from Christianity toward sheer deism. Others were helped in their vigorous attempt to recapture a larger sense of Christian values, especially those who had suffered from the extreme consequences of spiritual isolation. A particular kind of isolation which does not prevent people from "getting together," but which still leaves each tragically alone within himself. It may be that the communal keynote of the present age helped to crystallize that for which so many Protestants were seeking. Individualism is on the way out, and communal expression is coming in. The ferociously individualistic French Protestant is becoming, more and more, a figure of the past.

Some time ago a number of Protestant churches were federated and a common order of service put into effect. This was a great concession on the part of many of the churches. More recently, the first French Protestant religious community was authorized and a monastery established. The community is centered in Cluny, near the site of the once great medieval monastery.

I can almost feel still under my feet the stones of the Burgundy hill which I climbed in the cold of a peaceful January evening. I could barely see the path. The group of boys who had met me at the station, four miles from the monastery, were jumping around me in their enthusiasm and shouting: "See the light? It's up there." I could discern vaguely the contours of the manor which had been the summer residence of the old monks of Cluny. Abandoned during the Revolution, then occupied by people who took no interest in it for what it had been, surrounded by a village that is slowly being evacuated, the manor stands solitary, but still lovely, on the hilltop.

At the door I was welcomed by a friendly young mother, one of those who help to look after the children. The brothers, the children told me, were out trying their new acquisition, a car, a magnificent piece of junk. They had broken down, and one had returned to fetch a horse. The horse, the car and the brothers were still away, and that explained why they had not met me at the station.

I awaited the brothers in a simple and exquisitely paneled room which, because of the fuel shortage, served both as library and chapel during the winter. A beautiful old Bible was open on the altar, and a magnificent crucifix hung over it. To the left was a pulpit on which rested a page reproduced from an illuminated book and representing the Nativity. I should remind the reader, at this point, that I was in a Calvinist, not a Lutheran or Anglican, place of worship.

The brothers came back, with the horse and without the car. We had supper at a horseshoe table, and I listened to the continuous singing of the joyful brothers. Later we sat before the open fire and talked. I learned that in this first communal experiment by French Protestants there were men of scientific training, theological students, physicians, artists. They had suffered bitterly from the spiritual separateness to which French

Protestantism had led them. Gradually, they came to realize that their vocations lay in forming a community which would live in the world and to which each member would be bound by faith in Christ and by a minimum of common rules.

What would that involve—Roman Catholicism? Or a rediscovery of old truths which had been ruthlessly or fearfully ignored for centuries? But, even when misguided, the complete faithfulness to one's own self must bear fruit in time. It was a high moment in my tour when I listened to these men as they humbly related their spiritual rediscoveries. Anyone who knows the understandable but enormous intellectual conceit of the French Protestants can understand how deeply the Cluny brothers had to delve into the spiritual life to come around to such a humble state.

The Community of Cluny is comprised of two concentric circles, the Great Community and the Resident Community. The aim of the former is "to unite through prayer and work any Protestant intellectuals for whom communal life has become a vital necessity and ardent desire. Groups are formed under the different cultural disciplines with the aid of a director of studies, who arranges, stimulates and helps the efforts. The communal spirit fertilizes intellectual work. Every two months the Great Community holds a reunion for work and prayer. At times there are longer retreats."

177

It was realized from the beginning that the Great Community would not remain truly communal unless it were animated by the Resident Community, whose chief function would be to keep the Great Community constantly reminded of its duty to live up to its principles in the fullest degree. "Preaching by word," runs the community declaration, "should always be accompanied by example. The Resident Community, therefore, should strive to become the image of the Christian community, a vivid image with definite outlines, and thus should be more understandable to the individualistic consciences of our day."

The Resident Community, then, was introduced. It was deemed best to have two communities—not only because of the spiritual impetus that one could give to the other, but also because it was thought wise not to have the families of communal members live in the monastery, else it might take on the aspect of a lodging house. Again, while family life was an excellent thing for parish life, it would not permit the monastic community to fulfill its vocation.

These practical realizations remind us strongly of age-old Catholic procedures, yet the community cannot be said to have deliberately incorporated specific Catholic rules. They concluded that such a frame of life is a natural necessity.

Next, it became apparent that celibacy went hand

in hand with residence, and only those men who were called upon to remain single could join the Residence Community permanently. They do not take vows of chastity; they merely recognize that the single life is, at least for a time, a vocation which enables them to devote full time to furthering the Kingdom.

The Community enjoins a sharing of all possessions. "Those who live together must not be separated by considerations of 'mine' and 'thine.' Feelings of superiority or inferiority arising from one's degree of financial resources would be intolerable. All possessions, however small, shall be managed by the steward of the community."

The sharing of possessions is extended at Cluny to everything, including even intellectual, artistic and spiritual riches. Nothing is kept for oneself alone. "This sharing brings about a transparence between man and man. It does not mean an outpouring of self, but a limpidity of self."

These principles are so close to those of Assisi that we are not surprised when we are also told about poverty. But we should be surprised, and greatly, because French Protestantism has always been a religion of wealthy people. At Cluny the community recalls that Christ said: "Blessed are the poor in spirit, for theirs is the kingdom of heaven." "*Is*," not "*will be*," they point out: the only Beatitude where the result of the attitude is felt *now*.

The community members consider that in advocating spiritual directors they are acting in the purest Calvinistic tradition. This is a startling attitude on their part, and perhaps has some justification, but the whole question of spiritual directorship has been one of the main issues of conflict between Protestants and Catholics in France. If Calvin did favor such guidance, it has since made little impression on French Protestants. But it is an active principle at Cluny. Spiritual directors are carefully chosen, and then only after they have given unquestionable evidence of profound humility and exemplary self-sacrifice. The brothers are under no compulsion to submit to spiritual guidance, although in practice they do; they consider that they are actually obeying God, not the spiritual director through whom divine guidance is merely channeled. The sacerdotal character is not recognized by the Protestants, except in a few circles, and the authority of the guide can rest only on personal grounds.

Every member of the Cluny Community pursues his own vocation, but the necessity for a community rhythm is recognized. There is a Rule, and it is a simple one, like St. Benedict's:

"*Ora et Labora ut Regnet.*

"That your work and rest during the day shall be vivified by the word of God.

"In all things keep inner silence and remain in Christ.

"Fill yourself with the spirit of the Beatitudes: Joy, Simplicity, Mercy."

The day starts at sunrise, when the bell is rung. There is a brief meeting to meditate on the Rule. Then there is a liturgical service which sometimes, and always on Sunday, includes communion service. A verse for the day is read from Scripture. The entire morning is devoted to artistic or intellectual work, with some time taken out for manual labor. At ten o'clock a bell is rung, and the brothers stop work for a few minutes to meditate on the verse for the day. They meet at noon for lunch, which on occasions is observed in silence. Then the brothers are free until four. At six-thirty they meet for readings from the Old Testament and for prayer. Supper is eaten in silence. Evenings are spent conversing and playing music. Before retiring in silence, they meet once more for a reading of the chapter from which the day's verse was taken.

A full introduction to the liturgical life was published in 1946 by Max Thurian, one of the theological residents of Cluny. This book, *Joie du ciel sur la terre*, is the work of a man of great learning and profound thinking. He knows not only his Protestant authors, but also the Roman Breviary, the Missal and Orthodox liturgy. After a discussion of the historical, biblical and Christian basis of liturgy, he offers a full liturgical service.

The Cluny brothers are hosts of incomparable charm and simplicity, and they are ready to discuss with avidity the glories of old Cluny or the latest ideas on the state of the world and the possibility of Christian unity. They have visitors from all walks of life, including Catholic priests and monks and Marxist workers. By degrees they are acquiring abandoned houses in the village and getting them in readiness for members of the Great Community who come to live there during the summer.

The Cluny ideal, in which is intertwined so closely the necessity of guiding others toward a higher spiritual life, still is difficult for Protestants to understand. The idea of doing good to others is, to them, identified with satisfying the physical, or predominantly physical, needs of people. But a new concept has dawned among the Cluny Calvinists, and even outside Cluny there are retreat houses. One such house was founded on the principle that "our present age requires that some of us keep guard over the treasures of the soul, away from the tumult of the world. There must be a place of peace where we may listen to a voice which is not ours nor that of propagandists. . . . Celibacy is a necessary vocation for some people, a truth which we Protestants have not properly understood."

In Protestantism, then, as well as in Catholicism, there is a liturgical and communal renewal. The starting points are indeed different, and the roads traveled, but that the two forces are converging towards a mutual understanding and a common aim there can be no doubt.

One of the most effective general movements of contemporary French Protestantism has been the formation of the group called CIMADE. This is the Comité Inter-Mouvements auprès des Evacués. It was formed in 1939, and all the French Protestant youth organizations which were grouped under the CPJ (Conseil Protestant de la Jeunesse) participated. Their purpose was to determine what must be done for the sufferers of France, and to act among them as living witnesses of the love of Christ. The first requisite was to be *physically present* among sufferers. Material help would naturally radiate from their presence.

The CIMADE does not decide beforehand where its teams will do their work. They go wherever people are alone, and they mingle with displaced persons, deportees and the homeless. They make it particularly clear that they are not social workers, but Christians, who want to be present in times of emergency.

The CIMADE collaborates with the Quakers, the

Secours Suisse, Jewish organizations and the World Council of Churches. But at first they were alone, working without help. They sprang up when Alsatians, the majority of whom were Protestants, were homeless wanderers in the south of France. The teams of the CIMADE then had small cars, and they could circulate among the people and get them together into youth groups, Sunday schools and women's circles. After the armistice of 1940 most of these Alsatians returned to their own lands, but the CIMADE was faced with a much more difficult problem. The Germans had ordered the political refugees from Spain, Germany and Central Europe to be sent from their places of refuge to concentration camps in unoccupied France. On the heels of this order came the deportation of German Jews from Baden in October, 1940. According to a CIMADE report, "Ten thousand Jews, including some from maternity wards, old people's homes and insane asylums, were suddenly arrested and sent to France. They were sealed in twenty trains of cattle cars. The stationmaster at Pau telephoned the director of the camp at Gurs: 'I have here a line of cars from Germany for you. Judging from the shrieks I hear, I believe they are human beings.' "

A few weeks later the CIMADE was there at the gate, asking to be let in, under the pretext that they wanted to look after the Protestants in the concentration camp. They received authorization to come in for one day. Every day for a month the CIMADE members walked the five miles from their headquarters to Gurs. Their stubbornness won out. They were allowed to take up quarters in one of the barracks. They had to open umbrellas over their beds to keep the rain out, but at least the barracks building was large and could harbor many people. There were "fifteen thousand of them, men and women, without security, without human dignity, with no one to turn to. During that inexpressible trial there was one fixed center for many of them, the CIMADE barracks." Books soon arrived, then musical instruments. Many of the deportees were first-class musicians. Then the CIMADE noticed that the food rations were becoming smaller and smaller. They went to Vichy, and there they succeeded in having the camp's food administrator changed.

By that time, other organizations were helping and contributions were arriving from America, so that more and more persons could be saved from starvation and disease. In 1941 other CIMADE teams gained entrance to other camps, helping sufferers in Rivesaltes, Recebedou and Brens. The following year the organization acquired a number of houses, where they could receive persons who were under house arrest. The teams shared the lives of the deportees to a large extent, and their sufferings were considerable. Some paid with their lives.

In 1942 the mass deportations of the Jews began. Twenty thousand in unoccupied France were ordered to Germany. The French authorities had prepared lists of those who were immune from deportation: persons over sixty, women with children less than one year old, Jews married to Aryans. The CIMADE teams were there in camp, discussing every detail of every case. At first they managed to save about fifty out of every convoy of five hundred. They finally raised the figure to fifty per cent. Those whom they could not save they helped to escape. They made out false papers, working nightly in hideouts.

In one hideout, where the doors were closed and the windows blacked out, two members of the CIMADE sat on the floor, surrounded by cards and papers.

"Abraham Bloch," said one. "I baptize him André Bourgeois. Do you remember the color of his eyes? Here, make the police chief's signature."

"I'll rub the card on the floor," said the other, "so that it won't look like a new one."

This was a problem, indeed, to the Protestant consciences of the CIMADE. They found ample food for thought in regard to "literal truth." To their credit, not only did they meet the serious need of the moment, much as it might seem to go against their principles, but they never ceased contemplating their principles and holding to them to the maximum of their ability. "Innocent people are being treated inhumanly by a pagan power," they reasoned. "We cannot be Christ's witnesses before these people without even trying to save their lives. It is necessary to deceive the police. But let our actions serve as testimony to our final purpose, and do not let them demoralize our teams."

Outwitting the enemy, guiding the people over the border into Switzerland, moving ever higher into the mountains as nazi vigilance became more intensive, all these things they did. They even stretched their own bodies over barbed wire so that people could walk over them to freedom. They did not regard their mission as resistance work solely, but as a Christian testimony.

At the end of the war they undertook new activities in the same spirit. They now have several houses where they receive displaced persons and foreigners who cannot produce identity papers and hence have no protection under the law. They maintain barracks in bombed-out towns, such as Caen, St. Lô, Boulogne and Calais. They are present in the prison camps that still exist for collaborators, for they are convinced that, among the collaborators, there still is need of Christ.

As an example of the spirit that inspires the work of the CIMADE, a German girl whose family had been killed in the bombing of Berlin arrived at one of the

CIMADE houses after innumerable difficulties and adventures. She was alarmed to find herself among Jews, and more amazed to learn that they welcomed her. "I am beginning to understand Christianity," she said.

This attitude of selfless charity toward all is distinctive of the CIMADE. It is their trade-mark, and from the Christian viewpoint, an outstanding one. Countless French people, non-Christian and Catholic, have devoted their days to the cause of the persecuted, and have even paid for their convictions with their lives. The CIMADE teams are to be particularly admired for their refusal to allow their vision to be clouded by any partisanship. They have made an immense contribution to French Protestantism and the whole Christian renewal.

Another aspect of the Protestant renewal in France is called "The Outstretched Hand: A Bridgehead in Pagan Surroundings." The center is a house in one of the most desolate industrial suburbs in France. The dwellings are squalid, and there are no trees anywhere to be seen. The Sahara desert is more congenial. There is nothing to rest the eye, please the ear or warm the heart.

I climbed the rickety stairs to learn something of the "bridgehead." I was met by a woman dressed like any housewife and was ushered into a small room. It was a pandemonium of furniture, papers and other miscellaneous articles, as befitted the only heated room in the house. We hugged the little stove as we talked. Again, and as so often during my tour, I had the enormous experience of listening to the inner music of a human soul. The founder of the Outstretched Hand came of a well-to-do Protestant family. From the time she was a little girl she had been haunted by the chasm which existed between herself, her family, their Protestant friends, and the working class. As she grew older she became more and more disturbed, finally becoming a Protestant nursing sister. This did not satisfy her, nor was social work the answer to her quest. She thought of becoming an evangelist, but that was not the answer, either. The barrier remained. She finally reached the conviction that, if one were to leave everything and, without pay, were to go among the masses and bring the power of the Gospel to them—really living the Gospel in their midst—one might then find one's goal. She followed this plan to the letter.

The fineness of her spiritual awareness made it clear to her that she could not do the work alone, lest pride creep in and ruin everything. She decided on the necessity of a team. This was in 1935. While she might have appeared slightly eccentric to her family and to the Protestant Church, at least they did know about "calls" and respected them. But the team was conceived on a completely communal basis. The members would work for their living, pool their resources and preach the Gospel "at their own expense." And that, neither her family, her friends, nor the Protestant Church could condone.

Unaided, almost unnoticed, the Outstretched Hand has for twelve years been a daily presence among the poorest workers. It has shared their sorrows, joys and difficulties—a neighborly help in this forsaken district. In their spare moments the team members distribute New Testaments in the streets and homes. They have turned the ground floor of their house into a mission room for weekly meetings. A young Protestant theology student, a member of a very wealthy family, has recently joined the movement and is an apprentice in a factory. He is the first Protestant minister to adopt such a life.

Of late, the Reformed Church has awakened to the fact that the team has been carrying on effective Christian work for years, and has called for similar teams to serve in other parts of France.

The French Protestant renewal shows that some French Protestants have taken on their shoulders not only the burden of new ways of living, but also the facing alone of those great Christian values which have been so consistently denied through the years by their own church.

Anyone, meeting such people, must be filled with a deep humility.

CHAPTER TWELVE

The Great Return

IN A CROWDED FRENCH street I suddenly came upon a huge parade, headed by a big wooden crucifix and banners portraying St. Jeanne and St. Thérèse. Men were pulling a cart, on which was a white statue of the Blessed Virgin, seated in a canoe, and holding the child Jesus in her arms. Throngs of people followed, many of them barefooted, with arms outstretched in the manner of the crucified Christ. They sang and prayed aloud together. A dense crowd lined the curbs to watch them go by. Most of them knelt spontaneously. A few men remained standing and kept their hats on. From time to time a man or woman would leave the curb and impulsively join the procession. It was a scene from the Middle Ages. Protestants were shocked. Non-Christians were indignant. Atheists were digusted. Catholics might or might not have liked it. In the words of Father Congar: "I can well understand the feeling of revulsion on the part of Protestants. I am one of those Catholics who have to make a real effort to overcome their disgust before they can participate in, or even understand, such forms of religious practice. No one is bound to indulge in this variety of pious expression, and the Church leaves us as in many other things a wide range of liberty in such matters. But every Catholic should try to understand them."

This leads us to the theme of this chapter, the Great Return. Every four years there is a Marian convention in France. It met at Boulogne-sur-mer in 1938 and coincided with the third centenary of the consecration of France to Mary by Louis XIII. On this recent occasion an artist made a replica of the statue of Notre Dame de Boulogne. Tradition has it that in 638, the people of Boulogne, praying in their church, heard a voice saying: "Go to the shore. You will see a skiff without skipper or sailor. In that skiff is a Virgin, holding a child in her arms. Bring her to your church, and, whatever you ask her, she will grant."

Countless French people, including Charlemagne, St. Louis and Louis XIII, have prayed before Notre Dame de Boulogne. The original no longer exists, hence the replica of 1938. Four, altogether, were made at Arras, and they were carried in a cart through all the parishes to Boulogne. It was decided that one of the statues should be taken to the next convention in 1942 at Le-Puy-en-Velay. The idea was to link the two conventions symbolically. But the war caught up with Notre Dame de Boulogne, not far from Reims. The country was occupied in 1942 and cut in two. The Marian convention could not be held, but a pilgrimage to Le Puy was substituted. Some Catholic youths took possession of Notre Dame de Strasbourg, exiled in the unoccupied zone, and of Notre Dame de Boulogne in occupied France. Walking barefoot under unbelievable difficulties, they managed to haul the two statues to Le Puy in time for the pilgrimage. It was decided afterwards to move the statue of Notre Dame de Boulogne to Lourdes.

On December 8, 1942, Pope Pius XII placed the whole world under the protection of the Immaculate Heart of Mary. On March 28, 1943, the bishops, archbishops and cardinals of France asked the French people to offer themselves to the protection of her Immaculate Heart. In that day the Great Return was born. Its aim was to put the Pope's desire into effect. Every French person who was conscious of his Christian responsibilities was asked to consecrate himself to the Immaculate Heart, to come back with his whole heart and soul to Christ.

Nothing has yet stopped the Great Return. The faithful have traveled more than 45,000 kilometers on foot, carrying and wheeling the statue about. They have gone through countryside and factory town. They have survived the occupation and the liberation. There has been little violence, and then mostly because a few mayors, fearing there might be trouble, sent the police to protect the procession. This incensed the townspeople, who resented the notion that police were needed to make them behave.

The official publication of the Great Return has taken pains to keep clear the nature of this manifestation: "It is independent of visible signs. It can be accomplished by a simple return of the soul to God, by the desire for a better life, by a better consciousness of true Christianity."

In the spectacular form of its physical expression it provides a shock, leading people to take stock of themselves, confess, do penance and resolutely turn to the Gospel for their inspiration. These very things do take place when Notre Dame de Boulogne passes by. Ten million French people have offered themselves to Christ through their consecration to the Immaculate Heart. Their written pledges are housed in a shrine. There are many more who have not signed pledges, but who have been awakened to a new spiritual life.

Protestants have raised the cry of idolatry and superstition. Naturally, there have been cases of idolatry and superstition. The best of things can be misunderstood and misused. But the important thing is that the movement has turned vast numbers of people to God.

Skeptics have said that nothing will endure from all this sort of thing. It is an emotional mass reaction, they say, a psychological wave without permanent value. But, why should mass reaction not be used for a good end? Should the field be left entirely to the non-Christians, as it was in Germany? As to its enduring value, a great proportion will certainly remain faithful to their conversion; the emotional occasion for a man's conversion need not taint the essence of the conversion itself.

Other countries—such as England, Holland, Belgium, Italy, Portugal, Germany—have shown an interest in effecting a similar program. It has been suggested that a Great Return be adopted throughout Europe, even to the borders of Russia, where for centuries the Blessed Virgin has been greatly honored.

In the Paris area the 1946 pilgrimage culminated in a watch taken up successively by people of all trades. The great cathedral of Notre Dame was full for an entire two days. Another impressive demonstration took place in the sports stadium outside Paris. The entire diocese was represented and 120,000 persons were in attendance. The people sang popular melodies and recited the rosary. A play in dance form was enacted, following the rhythm of the Litany of the Saints. "The crowd invoked the angels and the archangels, and the patriarchs and prophets who were the human ancestors of the Messiah. They prayed to the Apostles, upon whose shoulders rests the Church. They prayed to the martyrs whose blood has stained the Church red, whose deeds were the first chapter in a living story, which goes on to the end of time." Then came a tremendous cry from the crowd in the night: "God of our salvation, help us." The people recognized as their own the gestures, attitudes and motions of the dancers, who symbolized Christian civilization. The choral leader called out: "Lord, deliver us from our passions and our sorrows." The voice of the people's response rose in the night: "God of our salvation, help us." The microphone boomed forth: "From hunger, which kills our children . . . from tuberculosis . . . from adultery, which breaks down our families . . . from war and prison . . . from lies which undermine the world . . ." And the crowd clamored: "Deliver us, O God!"

The figures of the great French saints were projected on a moving picture screen, and a short outline of their lives came over the microphone: "In difficult times they remained simple and true. They were not vanquished, because they allowed Christ to live with them, Christ, whose Sacrifice will now be celebrated."

The Cardinal Archbishop entered slowly. Two hundred altars were ranged around his own. Two hundred Masses—one Sacrifice—were offered simultaneously, to emphasize the unity of the diocese and of the Church.

In his address Cardinal Suhard told them:

"This living community, this deep sense of belonging, such is the joy we want to offer the Virgin, such is the great lesson we have to draw from this unprecedented assembly. The time has come when Christians are beginning to understand that they are and should be Catholics, that is, communal and universal. . . . At least, tonight you feel it: this stadium overflowing with your mingled presence is the image of Christendom. . . . The Church does not want any other gains. She is not seeking temporal influence or political power. The Church is not a party, a clan, a faction. She is simply the true, the only, family of all humanity. She would languish if she were to be limited to one territory, one country, one culture, one epoch. She feels at ease only within the limits of the entire earth. . . . Therefore, brethren, if you are to be apostles, your lives cannot be spent in isolating yourselves, in stiffening yourselves, in holding on to everything in order to lose the least possible, but in mingling, in giving yourselves, that you may grow and live fully. . . . You cannot succeed while alone. In our times everything is done communally. The cell, for the apostolate, is no longer the individual, but the team."

At the Communion of the Mass the officiating priests, all dressed in white, moved in unison from the altars toward the people. Eighty-five thousand persons received Holy Eucharist. The dancers returned for Thanksgiving. Boys and girls in long, flowing robes danced around the statue of the Virgin. The crowd accentuated the rhythm by clapping their hands. The statue was carried around the vast stadium, followed by the cardinal and the clergy. "Alleluias" rose to the sky. Handkerchiefs and scarves were waved by thousands of hands, and the whole assembly burst into the popular song, "Be our Queen, we are yours."

The vast throng moved homeward. It was well past midnight. There was no transportation. The people walked through the suburbs, through sleeping Paris. Sleepers were awakened by the sound of the immense shuffling and opened their shutters. "What is it? A revolution?"

Yes, a revolution. The only revolution.

Ecumenism

O N JANUARY 24, 1947, A Protestant friend and I attended a meeting of the "Night Watch for Christian Unity." There was a platform on which the play for unity would be performed. The hall was filled; we had to sit on the floor. A man spoke into the microphone: "Please rise. Our Christian pastors are about to enter." The door opened, and in walked a Protestant minister, a Russian Orthodox priest, a Catholic cardinal. The liturgical play commenced. There were several successive tableaux:

Prologue
    A. Dawn of the World
    B. Torn Humanity
First Tableau
    The Dawn of the Church

Second Tableau
 A. The Torn Church
 B. Waiting Stones
Third Tableau
 The Hope of Reunion in Unity
Epilogue

The complete play required instrumental music
by Bach, Grieg and Wagner, which was missing on this
occasion, but it proceeded without such accompani-
ment. Recitant, actors, Catholic, Protestant and Orthodox choirs, all played their part. The audience itself
was to give the responses. It was quite impressive when
we answered the recitant:

R. The flock dispersed
A. *Through our sins*
R. The sheep lost
A. *Through our sins*
R. The sheep led astray
A. *Through our sins*
R. The city destroyed
A. *Through our sins*
R. The tent devastated
A. *Through our sins*
R. The grapevine ruined
A. *Through our sins*
R. The vine torn away

A. *Through our sins*
R. The grapes picked here and there
A. *Through our sins*
R. The bride of Christ in sorrow
A. *Through our sins*
R. The mother who weeps over her forsaken sons
A. *Through our sins*
R. The unfaithful bride cast away
A. *Through our sins*

The audience then sang, after the choir: "Have mercy, Lord, on your separated sons. We have sinned against Thee." Together, the group recited the Lord's Prayer and sang "Alleluia," closing with a popular religious melody, the refrain of which is: "Cause us to be united, and abide with us, Lord, for you did promise it if we all love each other." The minister, metropolitan and cardinal gave short addresses, and the meeting was over.

The meeting was announced as a "very fraternal watch of Christians belonging to different confessions," under the leadership of their own clergy. In another town there was a concert for Christian unity, with Gregorian chant, Protestant chorales, Catholic songs and Russian liturgical songs, the whole assembly reciting the Lord's Prayer at the close.

Many towns have liturgical plays and inter-confessional watches for Christian unity. In one village Protestants and Catholics had not met together in four hundred years. Persecution had been particularly relentless in the sixteenth, seventeenth and eighteenth centuries, and resentment was deep-seated. In 1947, for the first time, the Protestants and Catholics came together to pray and sing in an atmosphere of trust, fraternity, joy and peace. As the official Catholic poster, sealed with an imprimatur, which advertised the Week for Christian Unity, said:

"So far as France is concerned, Catholics and Protestants acknowledge that they have much to forgive each other. Catholics, especially, should know that Protestants cannot forget St. Bartholomew's Day and the revocation of the Edict of Nantes. The part played by custom and political passion in a bygone day does not prevent them from being filled with grief as they look upon the crucified Christ. In full harmony with the spirit of Holy Mother Church, they find peace in expressing that grief."

The programs for unity differ somewhat from diocese to diocese but, in the main, they follow the same pattern:

January 18: Unity of All Christians
January 19: Sanctification of the Catholics
January 20: Sanctification of the Orthodox

January 21: Sanctification of the Anglicans
January 22: Sanctification of the Protestants
January 23: Sanctification of the Jews
January 24: Sanctification of the Moslems
January 25: Sanctification of All Human Beings in the Truth of Christ

Some seminaries are particularly alive to the subject of unity, and the future priests are made conscious of it in various ways. There are lectures on the Church in Russia and in the United States, with a discussion of the differences between the Latin and the Eastern rites. There is documentation about the Protestant ecumenical information service, with headquarters at Geneva. The press has been particularly active on the question of unity through the magazines, *Vie Intellectuelle, Cahiers du Monde Nouveau, Dieu Vivant, Etudes,* and *Esprit,* and through such books as *Protestantisme Français, Positions Protestantes* and the outstanding and much used work by Father Yves Congar, *Chrétiens Désunis.* Songs are sung in the churches, for the aid of various nations, and in their native tongues. Thus, "Nearer My God to Thee" is sung for the American Protestants; "As the Hart Panteth after the Water," for the Scandinavian Lutherans; a Russian prayer, for the Soviet. Experiments have been made in harmonizing the Gradual, Alleluia and Offertory to the polyphonies of the Russian liturgy. The *Sanctus* has been sung in Russian and the Hymn to the Virgin in Greek. In Paris a solemn Mass has been celebrated according to the Byzantine-Slavonic Rite, with Communion distributed under two species.

Since the majority of Frenchmen are Catholic, the initiative has rested with the Catholics to take the first steps toward unity. The Protestants will naturally proceed with caution, since they are a minority. But several decisive steps have been taken toward a better understanding, and a common ground has been laid on the basis of mutual desire for unity. However, at the present time French Catholics are more open and active on the subject than French Protestants.

It was in America that the ecumenical movement was started in 1908 by the episcopal rector, Rev. L. T. Watson. His mission was to strive for the unification of the separated churches. At the same time, Spencer Jones was collaborating with Lord Halifax for a closer understanding between the Anglican and Catholic churches, and he suggested to Mr. Watson that on the feast day of St. Peter the Anglican ministers should preach on the spiritual power of St. Peter's chair. Watson immediately replied that he approved, since he was working along the same lines. He wrote to the Catholic and Episcopalian subscribers of his magazine, *The Lamp*, requesting that they pray for unity during the week of January 18. For the first time since the sixteenth century Protestants and Catholics were praying together for unity.

Ecumenism has since developed extensively. World meetings have been held in Stockholm (1925), Lausanne (1927), and Edinburgh (1937). In 1933 the Russian bishops introduced it into the Orthodox church. Three years later the Synod of French Reformed Churches recommended it.

After its aims had been considerably purified, the movement was approved by Pope Pius X in 1909, and in 1916 Pope Benedict XV extended it to the universal Church. From 1933 on, the idea spread to more and more French towns. Naturally, the Catholic Church cannot officially participate in the conventions, since "she robustly affirms that, in spite of the mud cast upon her by her own children along her historical pilgrimage, she still is the only Church to have preserved the authentic, infallible apostolic tradition."

The Catholic Church did, however, send three observers to Edinburgh, without power to take part in discussions or to vote. Since then, French Catholics, without abdicating their initial Catholic position, have gone ahead on the path of unity with fervor, benevolence and intellectual keenness. The results are to be seen in the previously mentioned demonstrations, in meetings of student members of the three great confessions, in monthly theological reunions approved by the hierarchy and in joint radio discussions. In 1939 meeting at Lyon, at which Monseigneur Lavarenne, the Protestant minister, Rev. Ribagnac, and M. Zander of the Orthodox Church participated, was particularly successful, and a subsequent conference on "The Mystery of the Church and the Mystery of Christ," held by Father Chaillet, S.J., of the Seminary for the Syrian Missions, the Protestant minister, Rev. Rivet, and members of the University faculty, was broadcast.

It was made clear that the movement is designed for *unity*, not *union*. Union is exterior; unity is from within. Unity cannot involve compromise on dogma. Throughout the world we can discern numerous efforts toward the ideal of unity. The "Invisible Monastery," for example, includes convents, monasteries and groups of Catholics, Anglicans, Orthodox, Protestants and other Christians. We know that men and women have offered their lives for Christian unity. The ecumenical movement has many aspects. The French members of the movement want it made clear that they are not working for unity in order to band together against something, be it fascism, communism or any non-Christian ideology that might arise. Their mutual labors are the result of their awareness of what unites all Christians rather than what divides them. Error divides, not truth. The scandalous division of Christendom can be ended only when all members of all confessions consecrate themselves to objective truth.

The Orthodox Church is, in a manner of speaking, a meeting at the crossroads for the different faiths. At one time the Orthodox Church was expected to disintegrate, and some even hoped for a collapse. "In proportion as our whole world crumbles," says *Mission et Unité*, "so will Orthodoxy crumble, along with the social order into which she was incorporated. So it was thought. But the very opposite happened. Far from crumbling, Orthodoxy, within the temporal communist regime, found itself purified. In the first place, her priests and bishops were too inclined to be administrators and mix in politics. They were imprisoned and denied everything. Then, in poverty, nakedness, estrangement, they found something which was at once much purer and quite in line with Orthodoxy."

Of course, now that Stalin has made peace with the Orthodox Church, the danger has again arisen of her being used as a tool by a totalitarian state. While we should be perfectly clear on this point, the main thing for Catholics to do is to know the Orthodox Church more fully. Russia is no longer a faraway land to be comfortably ignored. She has taken a leading role in world affairs, and it is unthinkable that Catholics should give no attention to the destiny of one of the largest segments of Christendom. The Oriental faiths have an entirely different relation to the Roman Catholic Church from that of the Protestant faiths. For one thing, they have maintained the old hierarchical organization, Holy Orders and the other sacraments. In the second place, their doctrinal divergence from Catholicism is not considerable and is based more on misunderstanding than on fundamental incompatibility. Such is the view of Istina, the Dominican Center for Russian Studies.

The Dominican Center has dedicated itself to the discovery of points of collaboration. "Without denying the need for a revision of the historical conflict which for centuries has confronted the Christians of East and West," they say, "reconciliation cannot be affected merely on the basis of past circumstances." *

The Dominicans are bent on a "revaluation of the sense of the Church and its mystical unity." It is not unity of action that they are seeking, but "a deeper impregnation by Christian yeast of the principles by which the world should be positively organized for its own salvation." Their aim is not the absorption of Orthodoxy by Catholicism. "The aim is to bring closer and finally to unite Orthodoxy and Catholicism. It is mere

---

* A masterful study of the historical divisions between Roman Catholicism and Orthodoxy can be found in Father Dvoraik's "The Patriarch Photius: Father of Schism or Patron for Reunion," in *Prayer and Unity* (Oxford: Blackwell, 1942): those between the Eastern Churches and Orthodoxy in Stephen C. Gulovich, *Windows Westward: Rome, Russia, Reunion* (New York: McMullen, 1947).

illusion to expect Orthodoxy to evolve toward us without taking any steps at all in her direction." Fr. Daniélou, S.J., adds: "Orthodoxy has extraordinary liturgical power, which can powerfully attract souls living in the world today. She has a tradition of prayer that the Roman Catholic Church has, to some degree, lost. Consider, for example, the twenty-minute Masses in our churches! We have not established the right climate for prayer. In the long Russian ceremonies the soul sinks deeper and deeper into a state of prayer, creating a liturgical climate which is both appealing and strong."

With Russia coming of age, he continues, Orthodoxy may well become stronger, and unity may become more remote "unless we close the gap through methods other than those we are now using. God's plans are infinitely beyond our understanding. We must, first of all, pray. Then we must acquire awareness of the good in others, and recognize the fact that Catholicism has to take new factors into consideration in order to satisfy the various souls of mankind." Again, this is the Dominican conception. Istina issues a magazine, *Russie et Chrétienté,* and other publications in French and Russian. There is also a Benedictine Center which publishes the review, *Irenikon.* The Association of Prayers for Russia is well under way. The Dominican Fathers celebrate Mass according to the Byzantine-

Slavonic Rite, and have cordial relations with the French Orthodox Churches.

The latter, however, are for the time being handicapped in their work for Christian unity, because they, too, are torn by conflicting allegiances. Divergences within the Orthodox Church, however, are not so basically important as they would be within the Catholic Church. Nor have Moscow's invectives against the Catholic Church great importance insofar as the effort toward unity is concerned. Much is actually being accomplished toward a better understanding between Catholicism and Orthodoxy.

One great contribution that Orthodoxy has to bring to Western Christianity is the sublime conception, which they have stressed through the centuries, of the risen Christ. In the West the accent has lain, until comparatively recent years, on the crucified Christ. Both conceptions are strikingly needed, but today, after so much desolation, sorrow, crime and social convulsion, it is a good thing to take up the message of the Resurrection and embrace our Russian brothers in a vast *"Khristos voskrese!"*

Exchanges of methodological viewpoint are frequent, and the interest of most Christians to know one another better is taking constructive form. This interest takes many shapes. Frenchmen, both lay and clergy, ask what American Catholicism is like. "What are its characteristics?" they want to know. "Can we not know each other better?" "What about American Protestantism? Does it still coast along with nineteenth-century liberalism? Or are American Protestants disciples of Karl Barth? Is the Protestant group or the Catholic group more awake to the needs of the world and the tremendous responsibilities of Christians? What was the reaction of *thinking,* not sentimental, Christians, to the atom bomb? Have American scientists given that problem the same degree of study from the religious viewpoint as Teilhard de Chardin has done in France?" *

Such curiosity is a welcome sign in France, since her people have traditionally been too much concerned with their own affairs, to the exclusion of those of other nations.

"The walls of separation do not reach up to heaven," said an Orthodox bishop. The Orthodox churches often have been the channel through which Catholics and Protestants have met.** The outstanding Protestant weekly, *Réforme,* quotes from a speech by Marc Boegner, when groups of Catholics, Protestants and Orthodox met at the Roumanian Church in Paris: "The Orthodox churches have made it possible to estab-

* "Le Retentissement spirituel de la bombe atomique," *Etudes,* Sept. 1946.
** There is no direct problem of unity in France with Anglicans and Episcopalians as they have only a few churches for foreign residents.

lish contact in the West between Christian faiths that have been separated for centuries." The Catholic weekly, *Témoignage Chrétien*, has for long been on excellent terms with *Réforme*. During the Resistance, the Protestants, who did not have a paper, used the columns of the clandestine Catholic magazine.

Through one channel and another, Protestant and Catholic concepts are approaching to each other slowly and cautiously. It is strictly untrue, however, to rush to the conclusion that "Unity will be realized by the drying up of adverse currents." Father Naidenoff, S.J., is emphatic on this point. "I do not know," he writes in *Au Rythme du Monde*, "how to justify reasoning like that. It is decidedly harmful to our separated brothers. They are advancing with great strides toward a conception of their church which is identical with ours, even though, at the same time, they withdraw from us in their ardent determination not to bend under the yoke of Rome. We Catholics are guilty of the same contradiction. We lean as low we can, and then, when we have only to stretch out our hand, we haughtily straighten up."

But we have learned a great deal. As J. Kopf, O.P., has stated it: "We Catholics have learned not to be conceited just because we are the only ones to possess the full integrity of the faith. Rather, in that very conviction we are discovering a source of love and humility, and we have forsworn that hardness of heart which we showed only too often in our dealings with our separated brothers. We have opened our eyes to their treasures of inner life and deep Christianity. We are beginning to learn that we cannot demand everything of them. They refuse to turn about and retreat; they want to go ahead. This attitude on their part had displeased many of us. True, to turn about is to repent of a fault. Whoever personally breaks with the Church has to come back, like the prodigal son, to his starting point, at the very spot where the break was made. But our separated brothers cannot repent of a fault which they have not committed. At most, they can deplore their state and desire to emerge from it. They do not want to turn back, however; they want to progress, march forward. They do not want to abdicate what they have, but to acquire what they do not have."

Abbé Paul Coutourier, who has consecrated his life to unity, goes on to say: "Separated from one another by strong convictions, all Christians should, through greater selfishness, acquiesce more and more deeply in the ever-flowing, authentic inspiration of the Holy Ghost, who never ceases, within each honest soul, to cry to God: Abba! that is, Father! Only in this way will Christian groups renew themselves and be lifted to heights where the walls of separation are no more. In accordance with the faith I have in the Roman Catholic

Church, which, in consequence of its integral apostolicity, proclaims its own inherent oneness, we cannot, without blaspheming, ask of God the ruin of the other churches."

Father M. Villain, in *Emulation Spirituelle*, wonders whether "This spiritual emulation, generous as its aim may be, will not at least indirectly favor incomplete or irrelevant declarations of faith, which would constitute a grave fault on our part. We never," he says, "could approve these limitations and deviations in a declaration of faith. The one thing we do want is the increasing sanctification of all Christians. Do we not often take the wrong road in assuming such an apostolic attitude of conquest? When we are dealing with doctrine, let us learn how to mark the frontiers between what is essential and what is secondary. When we are considering discipline and piety, we have many revolutions to make. Does our faith in authority relieve us of personal study? Our Christian brethren might well think so when they notice how we have forgotten the way to the Bible, perhaps even held in suspicion that book which is a tabernacle of Christ. As far as our devotion is concerned, has it not become decentralized, hampered by routine and multiplication? Excess of formula means deficiency of soul. We race after indulgences without an ounce of attention or contrition. Are we not too 'quantitative' in our piety, too formal and oblivious to essential values? . . . Let us openly recognize our deficiencies, and let a more clearsighted charity teach us to discover in our Christian brethren those 'Catholic' values which have remained pure. Reforms are not a deviation from our religious tradition, but a deepening of it. Our Christian brethren can say the same for whatever reforms they might be willing, in the same spirit and purpose, to accomplish. Steady communal efforts of spiritual emulation will be necessary on the part of all faiths to renew the atmosphere of Christendom.

Such are the ideas of the French clergy who are working for unity. They have enormous good will and readiness to work, so that they truly offer themselves for "Unity as He wishes it and through the means that He wishes."

The movement for unity opens out into the immense question of the salvation of the whole world. Rooted in the scandal of a divided Christendom, it hints, in France at least, at a mission of vast proportions. "What Our Father wants," says H. Perrin, "is not so much our own liberation and happiness—there is, of course, personal salvation—but the big business, the essential business, which towers above time is the salvation of humanity and of the whole world."

This cannot be done by imposing upon the people of other countries or persuading them to adopt a foreign religion, clothed in occidental thought. Christianity has to be incarnated in the very fiber of other civilizations. Christ did not come upon earth to encourage the spread of typically occidental modes of thinking, feeling and expression. From the very start Christianity has made use of, and transfigured, the best in the various civilizations. It transfigured Judaism, from which it "flowers as Judaism's completion and explanation," as Danielou has expressed it. It has been clothed in Greek thought; it has relied on Roman legalism. It has drawn from civilization with which it has come in contact, whether Greek, Roman, Celtic or barbarian. In each there was a religious element which could be quickened, *as it was,* with its own particularity, just as there were certain elements which were destined to die. Some, such as ancient pagan superstitions, have not died yet.

Every civilization has priceless contributions to make to Christianity. Charles de Foucauld and Psichari pointed out that much may be learned from the Moslem's way of understanding and living prayer. The many books of William B. Seabrook have introduced us to a wealth of liturgical and sacred dancing among the native tribes in Africa. In India, the religious discipline has achieved a complete denial of the visible world. Authentic Christianity never destroys what is good. It makes it grow, transfigures it and enriches itself from it. It brings in new values which are essentially Christian.

What is not good is done away with, and the people are grafted onto Christ, "who knows neither Greek nor Jew —and, in the twentieth century, St. Paul's remark might be paraphrased further as "neither Moslem, nor Hindu, nor African."

French Catholicism looks toward future Christianity with a long-range perspective. It is working at this time for a Christianity which will fit the full dimensions of the world as it is today. This tremendous task calls for a high degree of intelligence, a warm heart and complete devotion to God through Christ. All the scientific and social developments of our age are examined without fear under the light of Christianity. The religious renewal is a surge from within; it is a rediscovery of traditional Christian values in terms of the present world. It is a rethinking of the problem of the whole man and of the whole planet in terms of those Christian values. The vigorous optimism of the French Catholics rises from their boundless confidence in God rather than in men. They have looked so far ahead that they see clearly that their position may, for some, end in martyrdom.

In conclusion, it may be said that three phases are to be discerned in the multifarious Christian effort in France. They have not revealed themselves in chronological order, but they have followed a marked direction, as in a Bach fugue. Voices have come in, intervening, progressing, furthering the architectural design through interplay of prismatic tones, up to a grandiose, breathtaking fulfillment. The three stages are the effort toward remaking Christians of one's brethren, the practice of Christianity as a communal affair, and the making of Christianity one.

These phases do not solely aim toward a rearrangement of the world, although they include it. Rather, by its very essence, the projection of Christianity is into eternity.

Works Quoted and Further Readings

L'Action catholique dans les milieux indépendants. Paris, JICF, 1944.

Augros, L. *La Mission de France.* Ed. des Annales de St. Thérèse de Liseux.

Au service de l'homme. Paris, JAC, 1945.

Bernard, J. J. *Le Camp de la mort lente.* Paris, A. Michel, 1944.

Bloy, Léon. *Celle qui pleure.* Paris, Mercure.

Bloy, Léon. *Le Désespéré.* Paris, Desclée de Brouwer.

Léon Bloy, pilgrim of the absolute. The life and thought of a great French writer in extracts from his works. Selected by Raïssa Maritain, with an introduction by Jacques Maritain. Translated by John Coleman and Harry Lorin Binsse. New York, Pantheon, 1947.

Boegner, M., A. Siegfried, R. P. Daniélou, S.J., et al. *Protestantisme français.* Paris, Plon, 1945.

Boulard, F., et al. *Problèmes missionaires de la France rurale.* Paris, Ed. du Cerf, 1945.

Cimade. *Reports.* Paris, 1940-46.

La Communauté Boimondau. L'Arbresle (Rhône), Economie et Humanisme, 1946.

Congar, Yves. *Chrétiens désunis.* Paris, Ed. du Cerf. Translated as *Divided Christendom: a Catholic study of the problem of reunion.* London, Centenary Press, 1938.

Couturier, P. *Rapprochement entre les chrétiens au XX⁰ siècle.* Le Puy, 1944.

Daniélou, Jean: *Le Mystère du salut des nations*. Paris, Ed. du Seuil, 1945.

Devineau, R. P. *Le Grand Retour de Notre-Dame*. Paris, Les Trois nefs, 1945.

Dumont, C. J. *L'Effort commun vers la plénitude facteur d'unité chrétienne*. Paris, Istina, 1946.

Etudes de pastorale liturgique. Coll. Lex orandi dirigée par P. Duployé et A. M. Roguet, O.P. Paris, Ed. du Cerf, 1944.

Fêtes missionnaires et populaires. Sacré-Coeur de Colombes, 1945.

Fumet, Stanislas. *Mission de Léon Bloy*. Paris, Desclée de Brouwer.

Godin, H. *La France pays de mission?* Paris, Ed. Abeille, 1943.

Godin, H. *Jeunesse qui reconstruit*. Paris, Ed. Ouvrières, 1942.

Godin, H.: *La Vie du Christ en nous*. Paris, Ed. Ouvrières, 1940.

Jeu liturgique: le mystère de l'unité. Angers, 44, rue Rabelais, 1944.

Kopf, R. P. *Veillée sainte pour l'unité Chrétienne.* Angers, 1945.

Lettres de Fusillés. Paris, Ed. France d'abord, 1946.

Loew, M. R. *Les Dockers de Marseille.* L'Arbresle (Rhône), Economie et Humanisme, 1944.

Loew, M. R. *En mission prolétarienne.* L'Arbresle (Rhône), Economie et Humanisme, 1946.

Lucien Marie de S. Joseph, Carme déchaux. *Problèmes sociaux et attitudes chrétiennes.* Carmel de Lille, 1944.

La Main tendue. Aubervilliers, 1944.

Messages de l'Aumonerie générale. Paris, 120, rue du Chreche midi, 1946.

Michonneau, Abbé, et. al. *Paroisse communauté missionnaire?* Paris, Ed. du Cerf, 1946.

Mission Bénédictine. *La Messe du peuple.* Paris, Ed. Nouvelles, 1946.

Mourier, S. *La Fédération universelle des associations chrétiennes d'étudiants et sa tâche oecuménique.* Lyon, chez les Maristes.

Naidenoff, P., S.J. *Au rythme du monde.* Le Puy, Mappus, 1945.

Perrin, H.: *Journal d'un prêtre ouvrier en Allemagne.* Paris, Ed. du Seuil, 1945.

Positions d'ACJF. Paris, Ed. Epi, 1946.

Positions protestantes. Par Pasteurs Casalis, Chaptal, etc., et les Pères Dewailly, Chifflot et Maydieu. Paris, Ed. du Cerf, 1946.

Pour l'unité du monde chrétien: le Centre dominicain d'études russes, Istina. Paris, 39, rue François Gérard.

Pury, Roland de. *Journal de cellule.* Paris, Ed. Je sers, 1944.

Quinze ans d'histoire. Paris, JEC, 1944.

Regards jocistes sur l'Evangile. Paris. Ed. Ouvrières, 1945.

Rousseau, Dom Olivier. *Histoire du mouvement liturgique: esquisse historique depuis le début du XIXe siècle jusqu'au pontificat de Pie X.* Coll. Lex orandi P. Duployé et A. M. Roguet, O.P. Paris, Ed. du Cerf, 1945.

Schutz, R. *Introduction à la vie communautaire.* Labor et Fides, 1944.

Sept ans d'histoire au service de la jeunesse française. Paris, Ed. Epi, 1946.

Tâches d'aujourd'hui. Lyon, Jeunesse de l'Eglise, 1942.

Thivollier, P. *Le Libérateur: vie de Jésus-Christ.* 1945.

Thurian, M. *Joie du ciel sur la terre: introduction à la vie liturgique.* Delachaux Niestlé, 1946.

Unité orthodoxe. Cahiers publiés par le comité interorthodox d'action oecuménique de Paris. 1946.

Van der Mersch. M. *Pêcheurs d'hommes.* Paris, A. Michel.

Villain, M. *La Communauté protestante de Cluny.* Lyon, Genebloux, 1946.

Villain, M. *Emulation spirituelle.* Lyon, chez les Maristes, 1941.

Villain, M. *Mission et unité chrétienne.* Lyon, Propagation de la foi.

Collections:

Cahiers pour le protestantisme

Centre de pastorale liturgique: Coll. Lex orandi; La Clarté-Dieu; La Maison-Dieu; Fêtes et saisons

Rencontres

Unam sanctam

Periodicals:

Cahiers de notre jeunesse (JEC)

Catholicité

Chef paysan

Commonweal

Dieu vivant

Esprit

Etudes

Economie et Humanisme

Le Grand Retour

Jeunes forces rurales

Jeunes gars (JOC)

Jeunesse de l'Eglise

Jeunesse ouvrière (JOC)

Le militant jaciste

Mission et unité

Le monde ouvrier

Notre revue (Fédération française associations chrétiennes d'étudiants)

Réforme

Russie et Chrétienté

Recherche de science religieuse

Le Semeur (F.F.A.C.E.)

Témoignage chrétien

La Vie intellectuelle

La Vie spirituelle